THE SUPER DUPER BOOK OF

101 Extraordinary, Exciting, and (Occasionally) Explosive SCIENCE EXPERIMENTS

By Haley Fica
Illustrated by Steve Björkman

Applesauce Press is an imprint of Cider Mill Press Book Publishers

APPLESAUCE PRESS

Thank you to Debbie Desjardins, R. Aileen Yingst, and Davida Margolin for their contribution to this book.

The Super Duper Book of 101 Extraordinary, Exciting, and (Occasionally) Explosive Science Experiments

Copyright © 2017 by Appleseed Press Book Publishers LLC.
This is an officially licensed book by Cider Mill Press Book Publishers LLC.
All rights reserved under the Pan-American and International Copyright Conventions.

No part of this book may be reproduced in whole or in part, scanned, photocopied, recorded, distributed in any printed or electronic form, or reproduced in any manner whatsoever, or by any information storage and retrieval system now known or hereafter invented, without express written permission of the publisher, except in the case of brief quotations embodied in critical articles and reviews.

The scanning, uploading, and distribution of this book via the Internet or via any other means without permission of the publisher is illegal and punishable by law. Please support authors' rights, and do not participate in or encourage piracy of copyrighted materials.

13-Digit ISBN: 9781604337501
10-Digit ISBN: 1604337508

This book may be ordered by mail from the publisher.
Please include $5.99 for postage and handling. Please support your local bookseller first!

Books published by Cider Mill Press Book Publishers are available at special discounts for bulk purchases in the United States by corporations, institutions, and other organizations. For more information, please contact the publisher.

Applesauce Press is an imprint of
Cider Mill Press Book Publishers
"Where good books are ready for press"

PO Box 454
12 Spring Street
Kennebunkport, Maine 04046
Visit us on the Web! www.cidermillpress.com

Cover design by Alicia Freile, Tango Media; interior design by Cindy Butler
Typography: Scala Sans, Special Elite, Ad Lib
Illustrations by Steve Bjorkman,
Supplemental imagery used under official license by shutterstock.com
Special thanks to Taylor Bentley, Annalisa Sheldahl, and Abigail Spooner.

Printed in China

1 2 3 4 5 6 7 8 9 0

First Edition

To the women of science who persevere every day, despite the setbacks. To the ones who do not always get recognized. And to the ones who do. You have paved the way for other female scientists and **we could not have done it without you.**

Table of Contents

Geology

Edible Rocks 12
Rockin' Rock Cycle 14
A Compass that Always Points North! 16
Rock Your Rock Knowledge 17
Make a Seismograph 18
Clouds in a Bottle 20
Who's Who in Geology 22

Astronomy

Sun Shades 26
Sundial 28
Dark Side of a Cookie 30
Phases of the Moon 31
Sun, Moon, and a Beach Ball 32
Scales of the Solar System 34
Why Does the Moon Glow? 36
Scientist Profile 37
The Big Balloon Bang 38
Who's Who in Astronomy 40

Biology

Water Filtration 44
Extract DNA 46
Naked Egg 48
Model Cell 50
Cultivate Bacteria 52
Number Estimates 54
Rainbow Rose 55
Dissect a Turkey 56
Who's Who in Biology? 58

Chemistry

Lively 60s Lava Lamp 62
Glow in the Dark Messages 64
Lemony Acid-Base Lemonade 66
Acid? Base? Red Cabbage Can Tell Ya! 68
Scientist Profile 69
Magnificent Mentos Gravity Geyser 70
It's Gold, It's Silver, No! It's Bronze! 72
Rainbow Colored Flames 74
Liar, Liar, Money on Fire! 76
Rubber Bones 78
The Periodic Table of Elements 80
Green Eggs and Ham 82
No Cooking, Cooked Egg 83
Density One by One 84
Instantly Icy 85
Egg Geodes 86
Geodes 101 87
Colorful Crayons 88
Playdough 90
Marvelous Milk Art 91
Ski Hands 92
Can You Steel the Heat? 93
Hand Heating Slime 94
Plastic Milk 96
Pocket Volcano 98
Elephant Toothpaste 100
CO_2 Bubbles 102
Peep the Marshmallow 103
Shake it like a Slushy 104

States of Matter 105
Can't You Believe It's Butter?! 106
Pop Pop Powdered Sherbet 107
Edible Glass 108
Peanut Butter Poles 109
Ice Cream in a Bag 110
Rock N Roll Candy 112
Who's Who in Chemistry? 114

Physics

Forever Wet Sand 118
Out with the Old Paper, in with the New! 119
Ooey-Gooey Slime 120
Water Rise 121
Dancing Slime 122
Super Spinning Candle 124
A Fork and a Toothpick Walk into a Yoga Class 126
Feverishly Floating Orange 127
Totally Tubular Velocity 128
Up and Around the Magnet 129
Table Top Spin 130
Magnetic Fluid 131
Crush a Can without the Hulk! 132
Egg in a Bottle 134
Bottle Balloon 136
How Much Water Can Lincoln Hold? 138
Jell-O in the Dark 140
Chladni Plates 142
Simple Circuitry 144
Lemon-Lime Power 145
Scientist Profile 146

Expanding Slippery Soap	147
Magnetic Train	148
Earl Grey Ready Rocket	150
Pop Corn on the Cob	152
Tornado Twister Tangle	154
Bucket Swing	156
Freezing Wire	158
Walking on Egg Shells	160
Sling Shot Catapult	162
Free Falling Egg	164
Rube Goldberg Activity	165
Mr. Potato Clock	166
Balloon Vroom Vroom	168
Series Circuit	170
Picky Pi	171
Solar S'Mores	172
Magnifying Heat	174
Candy Chromatography	176
3D Polarized	177
Static Lightning	178
Candy Crush Light	180
Rainbow through Water	182
Clear Rainbow	184
Rainbow Reveal	185
Mini Hovercraft	186
Electric Motor	188
Basic Binary Numbers	190
Pick a Card! Any Card!	191
Who's Who in Physics?	192
Index	196

WHAT IS SCIENCE?

That's a great question! Science is everywhere; it's the reason your microwave works, the reason that a struck match creates a flame, even the reason that your bottom doesn't fall through the chair that you're sitting on!

Science is all about having a question and searching for an answer. You form your hypothesis, conduct experiments to determine how something works, and study the results to determine how correct your hypothesis is. As the wise folks from *Mythbusters* once said, the only difference between science and messing around is writing it down!

We're here for the cool stuff! We want to see the explosions and color-changing experiments that make us think that we're performing magic from the convenience of our own kitchen! But the goal here is to perform science, not magic, so get yourself a composition lab notebook and take some notes! Scientists are always careful note takers because, well, every aspect of the experiment is important! Information that you may not think is valuable now might be crucial in the future. But if you don't want to write anything down, that's ok too! Grab your supplies and get going on those experiments!

WHAT'S NEXT?

I hope you're excited for what awaits in the chapters ahead! We will be exploring five different areas of science: geology, astronomy, biology, chemistry, and physics. Find out which one is your favorite!

Most of the materials used in this book can be found in your home, though anything that you don't have can be found at your local hardware store. All of these experiments are designed to get you to think about why stuff happens, so every experiment has an explanation in regards to the science behind it. Try this: think about an experiment after you do it. Try to come up with your own explanation, and see how it compares to the one in the book. That is the first step in the scientific process. You might not be right, but scientists rarely are their first time around!

UH-OH, SAFETY?

Ensuring safety is important in performing a successful experiment. If you are working with an experiment that uses heat, be sure not to burn yourself. If you are working with chemicals, make sure that you have an adult around. The same goes for any experiments involving fire. Breathing in too many fumes or getting copper sulfate near your mouth will NOT be fun. And under NO circumstances should you eat anything that isn't listed as being edible. We definitely don't want that. For the experiments that are edible, make sure that you're working in a clean environment so as to avoid ingesting any not-so-friendly chemicals. Lastly, science can get MESSY. Make sure you always have a lab coat or apron handy, especially for any experiments with food coloring.

NOW, GO GET ON WITH SOME SCIENCE AND ENJOY YOURSELVES!

Geologists study the Earth, rocks, and any form of terrestrial process that changes over time. That can include rocks, plate tectonics, climate change, mineral resources, oil, and even the geology of other planets or bodies. Geology even extends to the moon, as NASA is likely still studying the moon rock brought back by Harrison Schmitt, the first geologist on the moon, after his Apollo 17 mission several decades ago.

The moon actually has a lot of geological background. When you go out at night, look up at the full moon; you'll notice a lot of different colors and shapes. Back in the 1890s, a man named Grove Gilbert was looking at the moon when he wondered how the craters and colors were created in the first place. He hypothesized, and later found proof that supported, that other rocks in space called meteoroids hit the moon, creating the craters. Just imagine: a rock zooming toward the Moon, hitting it, creating an impact crater, and disturbing all of the dust and surface of the moon! It seems like science fiction, but it's not! It's real, and its geology!

In this section, you will discover how rocks form, why compasses always point north, and how to make clouds. All of this is stuff that geology studies in great detail. Think about the Earth and what makes it unique. A magnetic field, for example! We can use a compass because somewhere thousands of miles beneath your feet is a huge molten iron core swirling and turning about at the center of the Earth. This twirling creates a current (like a current that flows through a wire), which creates a magnetic field, which allows us to use a compass!

Here, you will become your own geologist; you will delve into research in a way that is similar to how science is done on a larger scale! Remember: science is all about discovery,

SO GEAR UP AND GRAB SOME ROCKS!

EDIBLE ROCKS

- 8 Oreos
- Large plastic bag
- Large bowl
- 1 cup chocolate chips
- ¾ cup mini-marshmallows
- 1 cup butterscotch morsels
- 1 cup peanut butter
- Wax paper

GRADES: 4TH AND UP

1 Place all of the Oreos in the plastic bag. Seal shut and smash the cookies into tiny pieces.

2 Pour the Oreo pieces into a large bowl. Mix in the chocolate chips, mini-marshmallows, and butterscotch morsels. Stir well. Add the peanut butter to the bowl and stir until the mixture is consistent.

3 Lay down a sheet of wax paper on a flat surface. Scoop out pieces of the mixture, mold however you want with your hands, and place on the wax paper. These are your sedimentary rocks!

What's Happening

Sedimentary rocks are created when existing rocks go through the processes of weathering, deposition, cementation, and compacting. In this experiment, your "existing rocks" are the Oreos, chocolate chips, butterscotch morsels, and mini marshmallows. Smashing the Oreos into small pieces in the plastic bag represents weathering, a process that occurs when a larger rock breaks apart into smaller rocks due to prolonged exposure to the rain and running

Form your own delicious sedimentary rocks using edible ingredients! You'll learn how they form in just minutes, though the process takes a few million years in real life!

Science Concept: Rock formation

water, among other things. Mixing the Oreos, chocolate chips, mini marshmallows, and butterscotch morsels together in the bowl represents deposition, which happens when rock particles are transported to a new location by way of wind, water, or gravity, where they form the basis of a new rock. Adding the peanut butter to the mixture represents cementing, which is when some mineral dissolves and gets deposited into the sediments, bringing them all together. Scooping the mixture represents compacting, a process made by everything getting pressed together. Finally, after a few million years (or a few minutes), you have your sedimentary rocks!

ROCKIN' ROCK CYCLE

Eat your way through the rock cycle! See how to make your own sedimentary, metamorphic, and igneous rocks!

- Wax paper
- 9 Starbursts
- Microwave-safe bowl
- Microwave

1 Lay down a sheet of wax paper on your counter. Unwrap three different colored Starbursts and stack them in the center of the paper. Fold the edges of the paper over so that the Starbursts are tightly wrapped. This will represent your first "rock."

2 Try to (safely!) smash the Starbursts together. Pretty difficult, right? That's because this is our "sedimentary rock!"

3 Repeat step one with a new sheet of wax paper and three new Starbursts. This will represent your second "rock."

What's Happening

We have made three different kinds of rocks: sedimentary, metamorphic, and igneous. Sedimentary rocks are mainly created using pressure, which we did by trying to form one thin rock in step two! For sedimentary rocks, sediments get deposited and, after a long time of compression can form a rock. Metamorphic rocks are created through heat and pressure. In step four, we did just that! Sediments are heated and put under very high pressure, causing them to come together

GRADES: 6TH AND UP

4 Place the second "rock" in a bowl, place it in the microwave and heat for 2 minutes. Remove the "rock" from the bowl and wrap it in a towel. Try to smash them together. Notice how easy it is? This is our "metamorphic rock."

5 Repeat step one with a new sheet of wax paper and three new Starbursts. This will represent your third "rock."

6 Place the third "rock" in a bowl and place it in the microwave and heat for 5 minutes, or until completely melted. Remove the bowl from the microwave and let cool.

7 Once cooled, unwrap the wax paper from the Starbursts. See how they look entirely different than they did before placing them in the microwave? That's because this is our "igneous rock."

Science Concept: Rock Layers

into one enormous rock! Lastly, we made igneous rocks. Igneous rocks are formed when magma cools and solidifies into rock, much like in step seven when we melted our Starbursts and peeled them apart from the wax paper! These three rock types form the rock cycle. The rock cycle demonstrates how sedimentary rocks can form metamorphic rocks, how metamorphic rocks can form igneous rocks, and how igneous rocks can form sedimentary rocks! This endless cycle continues on all of the rocks around us, but only takes a few hundred million years, so be careful not to blink or you'll miss it!

A COMPASS THAT ALWAYS POINTS NORTH!

Use this compass on your next adventure!

- Scissors
- Craft foam
- Red marker
- Needle
- Magnet, with labeled north and south ends
- Large bowl of water

GRADES: 4TH AND UP

1 Use the scissors to cut a circle out of the craft foam, making sure that the diameter of the circle is a little bit longer than the length of your needle.

2 Color one half of the needle with the red marker. Stroke the red side of the needle with the north side of the magnet in one direction, making sure that you don't stroke in a back and forth motion. Stroke the needle 30 to 40 times.

3 Place the needle on top of the craft foam and place the craft foam in the large bowl of water, keeping it away from the sides. Watch as the needle aligns with north and south!

Science Concept: Magnetic Field

The Earth's molten core has conductive currents that create a magnetic field, which permeates all around our planet. The needle, having been magnetized by your stroking it with the north side of the magnet, will want to align itself with that magnetic field, much like a normal compass does!

 talc
 rainbow pyrite
 violaine
 labradorite

 jasper
 molybdenite
 perovskite
 clinochlore

ROCK YOUR ROCK KNOWLEDGE

Do you know which of these rocks are sedimentary, metamorphic, or igneous? Ask an adult to help you find the answers, and then quiz your friends!

 anthracite
 bauxite
 barite ore
 tiger's eye

 chalcopyrite
 malachite
 wolframite
 cuprite

MAKE A SEISMOGRAPH

You need this

- Scissors
- Cardboard box
- Plastic cup
- Nail
- Long piece of string
- Pencil, sharpened
- Handful of rocks
- White sheet of paper
- A friend

GRADES: 5TH AND UP

1 Use the scissors to cut the flaps off of your cardboard box. Turn the box on its side.

2 Cut two small holes into the left and right sides of the box near the top and at the center. Set aside.

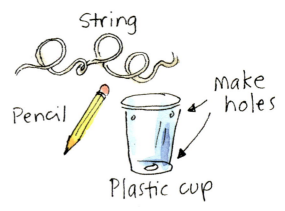

3 Use the scissors to cut a hole in the bottom of your plastic cup. Using the nail, poke two holes into the side of the cup, one directly across from the other. Thread the string through the holes.

What's Happening

This is a great model of what really happens with a seismograph! When you shake the box, it simulates an earthquake and the squiggly line is the record that measures the strength of that earthquake. When the ground begins to shake, the seismograph records the shake exactly the way that you did, only instead of a

Model your own Seismograph to see how scientists chart earthquakes and the motion of tectonic plates!

4 Stick the eraser end of the pencil through the hole in the bottom of the cup until the point is about two inches away from the hole.

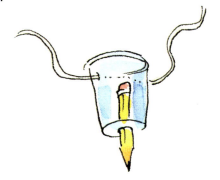

5 Place the cup inside of the box and thread the string through the two holes at the sides. Knot the ends of the string outside the box, making sure that the tip of the pencil touches what is the base of the box. Fill the cup with a handful of rocks.

6 Place a white sheet of paper under the pencil tip with it touching the end closest to you. Have one person shake the box while the other slowly pulls the paper toward themselves. You should end up with a squiggly line. Try varying the intensity of the shakes to see what happens to your line!

Science Concept: Tectonic Plates

pencil and paper it uses a complex electrical system that turns the shake into a voltage (meaning electricity) that gets recorded on a computer!

Earthquakes are measured using the Richter Scale! The Richter Scale is an exponential scale, meaning that a 7 on the Richter scale has TEN times as much energy as a 6!

CLOUDS IN A BOTTLE

- Empty plastic water bottle, with cap that has a mouthpiece

- 4 tablespoons warm water

- 1 box matches

GRADES: 4TH AND UP

 ### What's Happening

Water, air particles, and a pressure or temperature change are all essentials in the formation of a cloud. The process starts when water evaporates and rises into the atmosphere; a temperature or pressure change at this point causes the water vapor to cool and the air particles (pollution and dust particles) allow the water molecules to stick together, forming a cloud.

Clouds at your fingertips! Form clouds in a bottle one match at a time!

1 Remove the cap from the water bottle. Pour the warm water into the bottle and fasten the cap. Leave the mouthpiece released.

2 Light a match next to the cap and blow it out. Gently squeeze the bottle a few times next to the smoke. Close the mouthpiece.

3 When you're ready to release the cloud, open the mouthpiece and squeeze the bottle. You just made your own cloud!

Science Concept: Cloud Formation

Here, the match creates the air particles in the bottle and the warm water forms the water vapor. When you squeeze the bottle, a change in pressure causes a temperature change as well (this is called the Gay-Lussac law, and we will see this pop up in other experiments, too). When you release the bottle, the temperature in the bottle decreases and the water vapor inside cools down, resulting in a cloud!

WHO'S WHO IN

Marie Tharp

Marie was a special kind of geologist; she studied the ocean and was the first person to map the ocean floor. This was no small feat, considering how big the ocean is and the fact that she had to plot all of the data by hand. Working with Bruce Heezen, they used sonar to chart and map the bottom of the ocean! The data soon revealed that there was a continental drift in the center of the ocean. Called the Mid-Atlantic Ridge, this discovery confirmed the existence of plate tectonics. This revolutionized the way people thought of the surface of the Earth in the way that it functioned!

James Hutton

James Hutton is the founder of modern geology. His work was dedicated to the idea that Earth is constantly being formed, known as uniformitarianism. This states that all of the processes that happen today have always happened and thus shape the planet around us. In other words, the formation of nature is cyclical. His work led to the discovery that Earth is much older than originally thought, which can be determined by studying the erosion and sedimentation of the rocks around you.

Charles Lyell

Lyell's Principles of Geology laid the groundwork for modern geology as we know it. One of the first to believe that the Earth was more than 300 million years old, Lyell's work in the early to late nineteenth century served to debunk much of the accepted thoughts of the time, including Georges Cuvier's theory that creation and extinction was cyclical and that the theory of evolution was baseless and without evidence (more on that

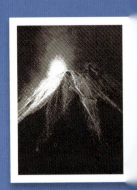

CHECK OUT THIS PERSON!

GEOLOGY

later). Among his contributions to modern scientific thought was the categorizing and re-categorizing of various historical eras, a better understanding of the mechanisms at work during an earthquake, and the concept of "backed up-building" in volcanoes. Of course, Lyell might be best remembered for embracing the mantra "the present is the key to the past," an argument on which his *Principles of Geology* is firmly based.

Harrison Schmitt

While their impacts may have been greater, few geologists can boast a resume quite like Schmitt's. A former U.S. senator and university professor, Schmitt is best known for his serving as a crew member aboard the Apollo 17. His was an experience that came as part of NASA's sending their first ever scientist-astronaut group into outer space and is, to this day, the only scientist to set foot on the Moon. He received the NASA Distinguished Service Medal in 1973 in recognition of his service.

William Smith

Of humble beginnings, William Smith spent much of his life the victim of plagiarism and a disrespect that led to his not receiving the immediate credit that his work should have earned him. Later known as the "Father of English Geology," Smith published a geological map of Britain, the first to cover that large an area. It was eventually dubbed "The Map that Changed the World," but it did little to improve his financial standing and, as a result, he was sent to debtor's prison in 1819. Upon his release, Smith spent several years as a surveyor until one of his bosses, who recognized him and his work, sought to gain him the recognition that he deserved. He was awarded the Wollaston Medal by the Geological Society of London in 1831, eight years before his death.

Astronomy is one of the oldest sciences: from the Ancient Egyptians to the Renaissance, scientists have always looked to the stars for answers. Much of what happens in space is to this day a mystery to us, so we continue to study the stars, galaxies, and even our universe using really big telescopes and computer models!

Unlike most sciences, astronomy has an ancient record, which we still use and build upon to create the models and theories that we have today! One of the oldest astronomical records is a Chinese record from July 4, 1054, of an exploding star, called a supernova, so bright you could see it during the day! Now known as SN 1054, or the Crab Nebula, this can still be seen using telescopes and continues to be studied 963 years later. This may seem like a long time, but astronomy abides by different time scales that are much, much greater than that of a human life. Our Sun is middle-aged and will last another 5 billion years before it blows up into a red giant!

Astronomy is also a way to look back in time! The farther away a galaxy is, the longer the light takes to travel to you. So, the light of a galaxy 4 million light years away would take 4 million years to get to us. This means that what we're seeing is the galaxy as it was 4 million years ago. As telescopes continue to get larger and larger our capacity to see farther back in time increases, allowing us to observe an increasingly younger universe that might offer us clues regarding the origin of existence!

In this section, we will learn about our solar system and how large it is. We will discover the dark side of the moon and how astronomers chart stars in the sky.

ANYONE CAN BE AN ASTRONOMER; ALL YOU HAVE TO DO IS LOOK UP!

SUN SHADES

- Cardboard box
- Scissors
- Tin foil
- Tape
- Thumb tack
- White piece of paper

GRADES:
6TH AND UP

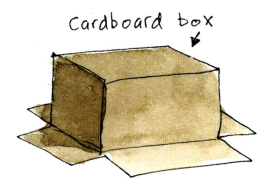

cardboard box

1 Cut a small rectangular hole in one of the shorter ends of the cardboard box.

Cut off flaps and cut hole in end of box

 What's Happening

When a solar eclipse occurs, the moon travels in front of the sun and blocks it from view. This makes the outer corona of the sun visible. The corona gives off harmful light that can really damage your eyes, so you

Have your own solar eclipse party using these Sun Shades!

2 Cut a piece of tin foil that is slightly larger than the hole that you just created and tape it to the inside of the box, over the hole.

3 Use the thumb tack to poke a small hole in the center.

4 Tape your white piece of paper to the inside of the box, on the side opposite the tin foil. During the next solar eclipse, align the pinhole with the sun and watch the white piece of paper!

Science Concept: Solar Eclipse

cannot look at it directly. That said, you can use the sun shades to view the eclipse! Using basic principles of projection, the solar eclipse is projected onto the piece of paper and you can see what is happening without damaging your eyes!

SUNDIAL

Who needs a watch when you can tell time with the sun?

- Ruler
- Paper plate
- Push pin
- Sharp pencil
- Plastic straw

GRADES:
4TH AND UP

1
Using a ruler, locate the center of the bottom of the paper plate and poke a hole in it with the push pin.

2
Draw the face of a clock on the plate. Draw a straight line from the center of the plate to the number twelve.

3
Using a sharp pencil, poke a bigger hole through the center of the plate. Stick the plastic straw through so that it stands eight to ten inches over the face of the "clock."

4
At noon, go outside and put your sundial down in a sunny place. Turn the plate so that the shadow of the straw aligns with the line you drew in step two. Fasten the sundial to the ground with pushpins if you're on grass so that it doesn't blow away!

What's Happening

Science Concept: Horology

The motion of the sun is the very foundation on which the 24-hour day was built, so it makes sense that tracking where the sun is in the sky is a great way to tell time! As the Earth rotates throughout the day, the shadow cast by the plastic straw moves, a result of the sun's position in the sky changing. This is how people were able to figure out what time it was before the modern clock was invented!

DARK SIDE OF A COOKIE

Learn the phases of the moon using Oreos!

You need this:

- 8 Oreo Cookies
- Moon chart

GRADES: 4TH AND UP

1
Twist each Oreo cookie slowly so that the frosting remains on one side of the separated cookie. If you mess one up, feel free to eat it after replacing it!

2
Looking at the moon chart, model your cookie and frosting combos as such: New moon, waxing crescent, first quarter, waxing gibbous, full moon, waning gibbous, last quarter, waning crescent.

3
Put your cookies in a circle shape and follow the pattern on the moon chart. The new moon should be at the top, with the waxing crescent on the right and the full moon on the bottom.

Science Concept: Lunar Phases

This experiment creates a visualization of each phase of the Moon, which is the product of a recurring cycle that completes about every 28 days. Full moons rise in the east at 6 pm, are highest in the sky at midnight, and set in the west at 6 am. New moons rise at 6 am, are highest at noon, and set at 6 pm. First quarters rise at noon, are highest at 6 pm, and set at midnight. Last quarters rise at midnight, are highest at 6 am, and set at noon.

PHASES OF THE MOON

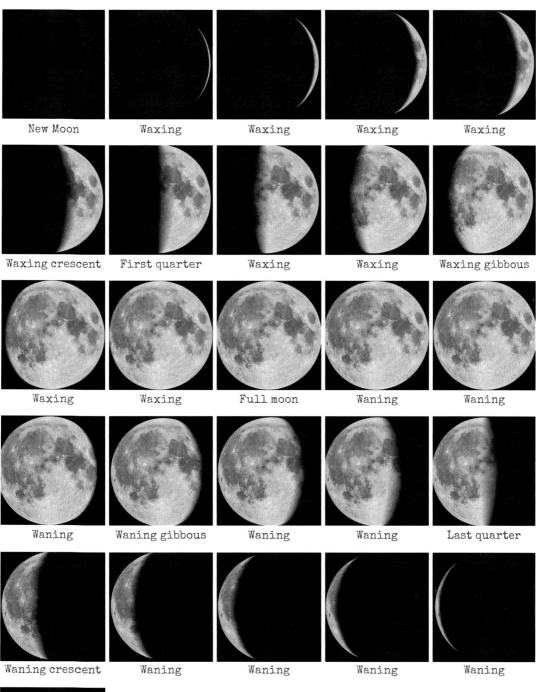

If you looked up at the sky tonight, what phase would you see? Is it waxing or waning? Have you ever seen the moon during the day?

SUN, MOON, AND A BEACH BALL

- Lamp
- Beach ball, inflated

1 Place a lamp in front of you and turn it on. Making sure that you have the proper room, hold on to a beach ball and fully extend your arms to your front so that it is placed between you and the lamp. You represent the Earth, the lamp the Sun, and the beach ball the Moon. Right now, the beach ball represents a new Moon.

2 Turn your body counterclockwise 45 degrees. Part of the beach ball face should now be illuminated. This represents the crescent Moon.

3 Turn counterclockwise another 45 degrees. Half of the face of the beach ball should now be illuminated. This represents the first quarter of the Moon.

What's Happening

This is what causes the waxing and waning of the Moon. The sun illuminates the face of the Moon and causes various parts of it to be seen from our point of view. Some of it is illuminated and some

GRADES:
5TH AND UP

Use a beach ball and a lamp to model the different phases of the Moon!

4 Turn counterclockwise 90 degrees. The entire face of the beach ball should now be illuminated. This represents a full Moon!

5 Turn counterclockwise another 90 degrees. The other half of the beach ball face should be illuminated. This represents the last quarter, which occurs when the Moon is waning.

6 Turn counterclockwise 45 degrees and you should be back to a new Moon. You've just finished cycling the phases of the Moon!

Science Concept: Time, Light, Planets

of it is in shadow due to the Moon being a sphere and being blocked from the Sun's light at various positions. The Moon is tidally locked, meaning that it experiences the same rotation on its axis as it does around Earth. That's why we always see the same face of the Moon!

SCALES OF THE SOLAR SYSTEM

You NEED this

- Register tape
- Meter stick
- Scissors
- Pen or marker

1 Use the scissors to cut the register tape to about one meter long. On one end of the tape, write the word "Sun." On the other, write "Pluto."

2 Fold the tape in half. Unfold it and, along the newly formed crease, draw a circle and label it "Uranus."

3 Fold the tape in half then in half again. Unfold completely and, along the newly formed crease closest to the "Sun," draw a circle and label it "Saturn." Along the newly formed crease closest to "Pluto," draw a circle and label it "Neptune."

GRADES:
7TH AND UP

What's Happening

You've just made an approximate scaled model of ou solar system! It is made up of eight planets and a dwarf planet: Mercury, Venus, Earth, Mars, Jupiter

See how big our solar system really is!

4 Fold the tape in half three times and unfold completely. On the newly formed crease between the "Sun" and "Saturn," draw a circle and label it "Jupiter."

5 Fold the "Sun" so that it meets Jupiter and unfold. Label this newly formed crease "Asteroid Belt." Fold the "Sun" to meet the "Asteroid Belt" and unfold. Draw a small dot and label it "Earth" on the left side of the newly formed crease. On the right, draw a small dot and label it "Mars."

6 Evenly space out two more dots between the "Sun" and the "Earth." Label the one closest to the "Sun" "Mercury" and the other one "Venus."

Science Concept: Astronomy Scales

Saturn, Uranus, Neptune, and Pluto (the dwarf planet). Now that you have an idea of how large our solar system is, you can better appreciate the fact that it is just a tiny fraction of the entire universe!

WHY DOES THE MOON GLOW?

Learn what makes the Moon shine so bright in the night sky!

You need this

- Tape
- 2 sheets white paper
- Wall
- Cardboard box
- 3 hardcover books
- Flashlight

GRADES: 4TH AND UP

1
Tape one of the sheets of paper to the front of your cardboard box and place a foot away from your wall. The paper should be facing the wall.

2
Tape your second piece of paper to the wall so that it is facing the paper on the box. Stack your books so that they're next to the paper on the wall.

3
Turn your flashlight on and point it at the piece of paper on the cardboard box. Make sure all other lights in the room are off. Look at the paper on the wall!

Science Concept: Visibility

The Moon glows in the night sky because it is bouncing light from the Sun off of its surface. The white paper on the wall is meant to show that the white paper on the cardboard box is bouncing light off of its surface.

SCIENTIST PROFILE
NASA INTERPLANETARY GEOLOGIST

Dr. R. Aileen Yingst is a senior scientist at the Planetary Science Institute. Currently, she is working on the Mission Mars Exploration Rover (MER) and the Mars Exploration Rover (MSL), but in the past she has worked on the Mars Pathfinder, Mars Polar Lander, and Galileo missions.

HOW DID YOU GET INTERESTED IN SCIENCE?
I don't remember a time when I didn't love science, especially space science. I remember going through astronomy books when I was just 3 or 4. **Part of me thinks I explore space because I couldn't join Starfleet!**

DO YOU REMEMBER YOUR FIRST SCIENCE PROJECT OR EXPERIMENT?
In 7th grade I did a research project on holistic medicine, where we studied whether certain colors make you calmer and stuff like that, and I came away with a lot of questions. I think it was the moment I became more of a skeptic, which is not a bad thing. A skeptic is someone who questions, who wants to know how to prove it.

WHAT DID YOU STUDY IN COLLEGE?
I majored in physics, but actually ended up going into planetary geology in graduate school.

WHAT DREW YOU TO PLANETARY SCIENCE?
I went into college with the idea that I was going to be an astronomer, and specifically chose a college that would allow me work on a professional telescope and do research as an undergraduate. Then, around the time of my junior spring I had to take a geology class. In the very back of the textbook was all the planetary geology stuff, and I read ahead and thought, 'Oh my gosh, this is awesome!' All of that work was really exciting to me, so I ended up going in that direction.

My first post-doctoral work after graduate school was with the Mars Pathfinder mission. I quickly found that mission work was where my heart was, so I put in a proposal and was ultimately funded to be a participating scientist.

WHAT IS YOUR FAVORITE PART OF YOUR JOB?
I love the data, but I really love working with the people. With mission work, I get to work with both scientists and engineers, who think and work very differently. It's by bridging that gap and talking to each other that we get the very best results possible.

WHY IS YOUR JOB IMPORTANT?
I go to work everyday knowing that 30 years from now it will benefit my kids - even if I don't yet know what those benefits will be. For example, the innovation that sent us to the Moon led to the development of cell phones and email! I know the work I do will ultimately make people's lives better, and that many people that work in science have that same drive. **We want our work to make the world a better place for everybody.**

WHAT ADVICE WOULD YOU GIVE YOUNG PEOPLE WHO MIGHT BE INTERESTED IN SCIENCE?
That there is no one who could not go into some type of scientific profession if they so desired. I am not a natural born scientist myself. But if you're curious, willing to ask questions, and not about to just take the first answer you see, then you can be a scientist.

WHAT EXCITES YOU ABOUT THE FUTURE OF YOUR FIELD?
In the short term, we have another Mars rover in the hopper right now, and if everything goes right it launches in 2020! But really, what's exciting about my profession is that there are no obvious limits.

THE BIG BALLOON BANG

You Need This

- Balloon, deflated
- Stickers

GRADES: 4TH AND UP

1 Practice blowing up your balloon a few times just to make sure it is nice and stretched out.

 What's Happening

This change in balloon shows and demonstrates the expansion of our universe (that's right, the entire universe!). In the 1930s, Edwin Hubble discovered that our universe is expanding at an accelerating rate! The stickers represent each galaxy in our universe; our galaxy is called the Milky Way. When watching the balloon expand, you notice that the space between each galaxy expands but the galaxy itself does not.

A demonstration on the ever-expanding nature of our universe!

2
Decorate the deflated balloon with your stickers of choice.

3
Blow up the balloon and observe how the space between the stickers gets significantly larger.

Science Concept: Universe Expansion

This is what happens on a much bigger scale in the universe. Space itself is expanding, but galaxies are not because gravity keeps holding them together!

What causes this expansion of the universe is called dark energy and it makes up about 68% of the universe! Dark matter (matter we cannot see but we know is there) makes up about 27%, while normal matter (the tables, chairs, and all the stuff we interact with everyday) only makes up about 5% of the universe. Imagine how much stuff we can't see!

WHO'S WHO IN

Edwin Hubble

Edwin Hubble was one of the world's most prominent astronomers. Born in 1889, he used various telescopes to study the cosmos, which led to his discovering that the universe is expanding. Called Hubble's Law, he saw that distant galaxies were moving at accelerated speeds. He performed a redshift experiment that allowed him to determine the galaxy's speed and velocity and found that the universe is constantly expanding!

Vera Rubin

Vera Rubin was studying the rotations of galaxies in the 1960s and 70s when she discovered the existence of dark matter, still one of science's biggest mysteries. She noticed that the stars on the outside of the galaxy were traveling at the same speed as the stars in the middle of the galaxy. This was seen as rather shocking, as the concept of Newtonian gravity led to the belief that the stars on the outside would be rotating at a much slower rate than the stars on the inside. She came to the conclusion that there was matter on the outer edges of the galaxy that we couldn't see and, fittingly, called it dark matter. This dark matter causes the rim of the galaxy to travel really fast, speeding up the rotation.

Johannes Kepler

Kepler is one of the original giants in astronomy! A major player in the 17th-century scientific revolution, Kepler is best remembered

CHECK OUT THIS PERSON!

ASTRONOMY

for his laws of planetary motion. An improvement on Copernicus' model, he was able to use his background as a mathematician to come up with three rules that describe the motion of planets around the Sun. His laws served as the partial basis on which Isaac Newton's universal gravitation theory was developed!

Carl Sagan

A co-narrator on the original *Cosmos: A Personal Voyage* television series (which has been seen by over 500 million people!),  Sagan remains one of the faces of modern astronomy. His interest in the prospects of extraterrestrial life led to his being the first person to ever assemble and send a physical message into space. They were known as the Voyager Golden Record and the Pioneer Plaque, and they had the potential to be understood by extraterrestrial intelligence. Sagan was also responsible for correctly hypothesizing that the greenhouse effect could be used to calculate the high surface temperatures of Venus.

Edmond Halley

A seventeenth- and eighteenth-century English astronomer, mathematician, meteorologist and physicist, Halley was the second Astronomer Royal in Britain. The title was well earned; among his achievements was 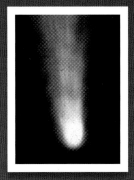 accurately computing the orbit of Halley's Comet. In fact, the comet was named after him!

THE CONCEPT OF EVOLUTION...

...was theorized by a man named Charles Darwin, one of the most important figures in the advancement of the study of biology. After studying animals and birds in an isolated area over a period of time, Darwin discovered that all living things evolved from a common ancestor. This means that you and a banana evolved from the same organism! Slowly but surely, certain kingdoms of organisms began to differentiate themselves: plants, animals, protists, fungi, archaebacterial, and eubacteria. Each of these kingdoms then began to evolve, creating all the living organisms you see (and don't see) today!

Biology has a detailed organizational system that starts at the top. Biologists classify organisms based on their general characteristics into the following: Domain, Kingdom, Phylum, Class, Order, Family, Genus, and Species (here's a little trick for remembering the order: Dear King Phillip Came Over for Good Soup). The domain represents the beginning of the organizational process and begins with the largest and broadest qualifier: are you an organism with more than one cell, or are you a single-celled organism? The classifications get more and more specific as you move along, until you're left with one, specific kind of animal. For example, all smooth hammerhead sharks have the same scientific name: *Sphyrna zygaena*, where *Sphyrna* is the genus and *zygaena* is the species. These names are different for every single living organism out there!

Cells and living organisms are everywhere; in fact, you have more living organisms in your body than cells actually belonging to you! We are hosts for all sorts of bacteria and organisms and they, for the most part, do us a lot of good! You can digest food because of the beneficial bacteria in your stomach (not all small bacteria are bad), but eating something bad can introduce harmful bacteria into your body (again, bacteria is everywhere).

You are about to embark on a journey into the world of biology. You will witness firsthand how body systems work and will extract and study the DNA of a strawberry, which is more closely related to you than you think! Biology studies living organisms: bacteria, plants, dogs, cats, sharks, even humans! We're going to start with the fundamental basis of all life on here on Earth, water, and eventually move into macro-biology, like how biologists count the members of a population without counting all of the animals.

WATER FILTRATION

- Scissors
- Plastic water bottle
- Coffee filter
- Activated charcoal
- Gravel
- Sand
- Glass cup
- Pond or dirt water

GRADES:
6TH AND UP

coffee filter

1 Use the scissors to cut the bottom off of your plastic water bottle. Holding it bottom up, place and secure a coffee filter in the neck of the bottle

 Science Concept: Life, Water

This is the basis of how we get clean water to your house. Everything that comes out of a faucet is cleaned through filtration before you drink it! Water is the basis of life and one of the many things needed in order for almost all life to survive. In fact, when looking for life in our solar system, water is the number one thing scientists look for in order to determine if a planet is habitable or not.

Filtering out the black particles in water is essential for us to have good clean water that is safe to drink! Learn the basics of how we filter water.

2 Add one inch of activated charcoal to the bottle, followed by 1 inch of gravel, 3 inches of sand, and more gravel until it's about an inch away from the new top of the bottle.

3 Place the neck of the bottle in a narrow glass so that it can stand on its own. Add about half a cup of the gross pond or dirt water to your filtration system and see how successful you are in filtering out the particles!

EXTRACT DNA

- Isopropyl alcohol (rubbing alcohol)
- 2 strawberries, stems and leaves removed
- Plastic bag
- 2 cups
- ½ cup water
- 2 tablespoons liquid dish soap
- 1 teaspoon salt
- Cheesecloth
- Chopstick

GRADES: 8TH AND UP

1 Place the rubbing alcohol into the freezer.

2 Add the strawberries to your plastic bag and mash them up. Set aside.

3 In a cup, mix together the water, liquid dish soap, and salt, making sure that the salt dissolves. This will serve as our DNA extraction mixture.

4 Add 1 ½ tablespoons of the DNA extraction mixture to the strawberry bag and continue to smash, being sure to avoid making too many bubbles in the process.

 ## What's Happening

The white strands that you pulled out of the strawberry is its actual DNA! DNA is in every living organism, from you to a blade of grass. We used strawberries here because they're octoploids, meaning that they have eight copies of chromosomes. Chromosomes are where DNA is stored and we humans have two of them, which

See what makes a strawberry a strawberry by using a few easy ingredients!

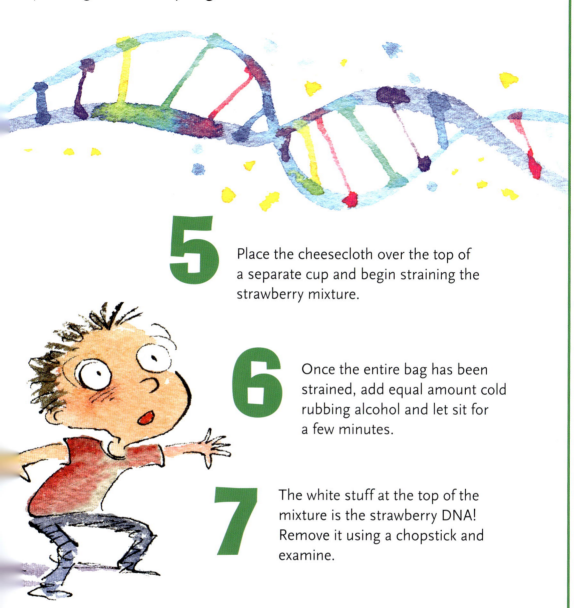

5 Place the cheesecloth over the top of a separate cup and begin straining the strawberry mixture.

6 Once the entire bag has been strained, add equal amount cold rubbing alcohol and let sit for a few minutes.

7 The white stuff at the top of the mixture is the strawberry DNA! Remove it using a chopstick and examine.

Science Concept: DNA Extraction

makes us diploids. So, obviously, we can extract more DNA using the strawberries!

All aspects of this experiment are essential to the process. The soap helps dissolve the cell membranes of the strawberry, the salt breaks up the proteins that hold the DNA together, and the rubbing alcohol helps to solidify the DNA. DNA is really small, but you can start to see it as it clumps together!

NAKED EGG

- Several eggs
- A tall glass
- Vinegar
- Spoon

GRADES: 5TH AND UP

Science Concept: Osmosis

Vinegar contains acetic acid, which dissolves the calcium carbonate of the eggshell. The egg gets larger during this experiment because of osmosis. The water in the vinegar is absorbed through the egg's membrane. To see osmosis in action, place your egg in cornstarch overnight. Cornstarch will contain less water than the egg does, and as a result the water will pass out of the egg's membrane and into the cornstarch, making it smaller.

Use vinegar to remove the shell from an egg!

1 Place your eggs into the tall glass and fill with just enough vinegar to cover the tops of your eggs. Let sit for 24 hours.

2 After 24 hours, spoon out the eggs and pour out the vinegar. Be careful not to puncture the eggs! Put the eggs back into the glass, replace the vinegar and let sit for another 24 hours.

3 After 24 hours, spoon out the eggs again and rinse them carefully. You now have eggs without shells!

MODEL CELL

- Boxed cake mix
- Three bowls
- White icing
- Green, blue, and yellow food colorings
- Air Heads Xtremes
- Green and red jelly beans
- Gummy worms
- Gummy Life Savers
- Sprinkles

GRADES: 8TH AND UP

1
Bake the cake according to the instructions on the box. Once baked, let the cake cool completely.

2
Split the icing into three bowls: the first bowl should have enough frosting to cover the top of your cake, the second bowl should have enough frosting to cover the sides of your cake, and the third needs only 4 tablespoons of frosting.

3
Mix green food coloring into the first bowl, blue food coloring into the second bowl, and yellow food coloring to the third bowl.

What's Happening

Each candy has a meaning and represents a different part of the cell:

Yellow icing:
Nucleus, where all the DNA is stored for the cell

Green icing:
Cytoplasm, the substance that is inside the cell

Blue icing:
Cell membrane, holds the cell together and aims to protect and enclose the cell

Your body has lots of cells, and those cells have lots of organelles! Make a cake showing how all of these organelles work together!

4 Spread the green frosting on to the top and the side of the cake. This represents the cytoplasm. Spread the blue frosting along the sides of the cake, which will represent the cell membrane. Add the yellow frosting to the center of the cake. This represents the nucleus, where all of the DNA is stored!

5 Place a few flat Air Heads Xtremes on the side of the cake. Add the rest of the candies to the top of the cake, grouping each candy variation together. Take a picture and enjoy the cake!

Science Concept: Cells

Air Head Xtremes: Rough endoplasmic reticulum, they take the protein created by the ribosomes to the Golgi apparatus

Gummy worms: Golgi apparatus, simple proteins are made into larger and much more complex proteins

Life Savers: Vacuoles, stores water and other things for the cell

Red jelly beans: Smooth endoplasmic reticulum, stores the lipids that make the cell membrane

Green jelly beans: Mitochondria, the powerhouse of the cell and creates the energy for the cell

Sprinkles: Ribosomes, create the proteins of the cell

CULTIVATE BACTERIA

Cultivate the kind of germs that hang out on your phone or on your door knob!

You Need This

- Gloves
- Clear goggles
- 1 teaspoon agar
- ½ cup hot water
- Microwave safe container
- Microwave
- 4 petri dishes
- Marker
- 4 cotton swabs
- 4 plastic bags

1 Put on your gloves and clear goggles. Remember, safety is important!

2 Mix together the agar and hot water in the microwave safe container and heat for four minutes, or until the mixture reaches its boiling point. Turn the microwave off and let the mixture cool for about 6 minutes.

3 Carefully remove the lids of the petri dishes, being careful not to touch the insides with your hands. Carefully pour the agar mixture into each dish until they're all about half full. Place the lids back on to the dishes, leaving it partially open to allow the heat to escape.

 Science Concept: Bacteria

The agar mixture is a great way to grow bacteria, as it is nutritional and helps them to multiply in your petri dish. You can see the bacteria because they are concentrated in one area. Much like the DNA, bacteria are too small to see on their own, but when there are millions and millions of them they are much easier to see!

GRADES: 8TH AND UP

4 Use a clean cotton swab to swab an area that you want to test! Remove the lid from one of the dishes and roll the end of the cotton swab along the top of the hardened agar mixture. Dispose of the cotton swab and secure the lid to the dish, labeling the top with the time, date, and area tested. Repeat this process three more times, testing a different area each time.

5 Place each petri dish in a baggie and store somewhere warm and dark, an area that is conducive to bacteria growth. Do not open the petri dishes from this point forward, as the bacteria that grows can be very harmful!

6 Check on the dishes every day until you start to see some significant growth, which should begin to take place after a day or two!

NUMBER ESTIMATES

Determine the amount of candies the same way biologists determine animals in a given ecosystem.

YOU NEED this

- At least 40 pieces of assorted candy
- Large plastic bag
- Marker
- Paper

GRADE: 5TH AND UP

1 Combine all of your candy into one large plastic bag, making sure that you have at least 40 pieces all together. This will represent your population.

2 Shake the bag. Close your eyes and pull out ten pieces of candy. Use the marker to draw a line on each piece of candy before returning them to the bag.

3 Shake the bag again. Close your eyes and pull out a handful of candy. This represents the recapture. Record the number of candies pulled and which of those have marker on them. Return the candy to the bag.

4 Repeat step three until you've recorded ten trials. Total the number of candies grabbed and the number of markered candies. Plug those totals into the following formula: population size = (total candies grabbed x number of markered candies grabbed)/ (total number of markered candies). This will give you the total population size estimate.

Science Concept: Biology Tagging

This is one way biologists measure animal population sizes. They capture a few animals of the same species and tag them with something visible. They then recapture the same species and see how many of them are marked. After several trials, biologists are able to determine the population size for that species. This technique is especially important because it can show the change in a population size. This allows them to see how something like a drought or a predator is affecting that species.

RAINBOW ROSE

Use the systems of a rose to turn a white rose into a rainbow!

- **White rose**
- **Ruler**
- **Scissors**
- **Water**
- **Red, blue, and yellow food coloring**
- **3 plastic bags**
- **3 rubber bands**

GRADE: 5TH AND UP

1
The stem of the rose should be about one foot long, so use scissors to trim if necessary.

2
Use the scissors to split the base of the stem into three lengthwise segments, four inches each.

3
Add six tablespoons of water and twenty drops of dye to each plastic bag. Put each split stem into a separate bag and secure them using a rubber band. Place the rose and the plastic bags somewhere that will allow them to stand straight up on their own. You should see the petals of the rose change color after a day or two!

Science Concept: Osmosis

The rose will bring up the food coloring along with the water through its xylem, which then travels through the plant's systems and capillaries. The petals change color because of the food coloring!

DISSECT A TURKEY

- Rubber gloves
- Knife
- Whole, raw turkey
- Paper plate

GRADES:
8TH AND UP

1 Put on your rubber gloves. Check to see if the innards, or "giblets," have already been removed (they will be in a bag inside the cavity of the bird). If not, put on your rubber gloves, and then cut the turkey open to remove the them.

2 You should have five or six giblets; the long hard piece is the neck.

3 Let's identify the other giblets! The heart is about an inch around and looks similar to a human heart. It should be about the size of the first digit of your thumb.

4 The liver is a deep reddish-brown and is soft to the touch. The gizzard has two oval shaped parts attached to it by some whitish tissue.

5 Put each giblet on a paper plate and use the knife to cut each in half. Observe internal structures of each.

Study the internal organs that allow the turkey's body to function!

What's Happening   Science Concept: Organ Function

The heart pumps blood throughout the turkey; the gizzard is used for digesting food and has thick walls to accommodate having to break up food eaten by an animal without any teeth; the liver stores nutrients in the body and regulates the turkey's blood; and the neck is exactly that!

WHO'S WHO IN

Rosalind Franklin

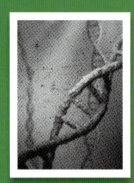

Rosalind Franklin, best known for discovering DNA's double helix structure, was born in Britain and received her doctorate from Cambridge in 1945. After a brief stint in Paris, Franklin returned to London to work with John Randall. It was there that she was given a DNA project that had been all but abandoned, which culminated in her utilizing techniques she had learned while in France to capture x-ray images of the DNA structure. Though her findings were stolen from her, she remains a fixture in the history of modern biology. Without her pioneering work with DNA, we wouldn't be where we are today in terms of our knowledge in regards to gene transfers and DNA functions. After her death of ovarian cancer at the age of 37, her research group was awarded the Nobel Prize in Chemistry.

Alfred Russel Wallace

Wallace conducted extensive fieldwork throughout his career, from the Amazon River to the Malay Archipelago, and is known primarily as being the "father of biogeography" as a result. Biogeography is the study of the geographical distribution of animal species, a subject in which Wallace was well versed; he was able to separate the Indonesian archipelago based on the geographical descent of its animal inhabitants. Wallace is also remembered as being a leading evolutionary thinker, as he conceived the theory that natural selection was the mechanism through which evolution occurred. In fact, he had some of his writing published with Charles Darwin's in 1858!

Alexander Fleming

A Scottish biologist, botanist and pharmacologist, Fleming's recognition is as extensive as anybody's during

> CHECK OUT THIS PERSON!

BIOLOGY

the 20th century. He was awarded a share of the Nobel Prize in Physiology or Medicine in 1945 for his discovering the world's first antibiotic substance (Penicillin G), was knighted in 1944 for his scientific achievements, was named in *Time* magazine's list of the 100 Most Important People of the 20th century, was selected in a 2002 BBC poll as being one of the 100 Greatest Britons, and was selected third in a 2009 "greatest Scot" poll. His discovery would go on to shape modern medicine as we know it, kicking off a period that would see the greatest year to year increase in life spans in civilized history.

Stephen Jay Gould

Another significant figure in the world of evolution, Gould spent a lot of his career working at the American Museum of Natural History and teaching at Harvard University. He's best known for challenging the phyletic gradualism theory, which stated that evolutionary change moves at a pretty consistent rate and that a consistent and gradual change can be seen in the fossil record. Gould rejected this idea; rather, he proposed that branching evolution took place, which was a long period of stability followed by brief periods of branching evolution.

Gregor Mendel

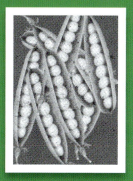

Born in the Austrian Empire, Gregor Mendel is known as the father of genetics. His research mainly revolved around various different pea plants, each of which had a different pod shape, color, seed shape, and height. He bred these plants to determine how their offspring would look. He coined the terms recessive and dominant traits to describe what kind of traits would be passed down to the younger generation of plants. There are two spots, so to speak, for traits to get passed down. A dominant trait means that if one of the two spots has that sort of description it will automatically show up. A recessive trait means that you need both spots to be the same in order for it to show up. For example, having freckles is a dominant trait, while having blue eyes is recessive. This kind of thinking and discovery was independently observed by about three other people before it was widely accepted and helped to usher in the current thinking in the genetics field!

CHEMISTRY HAS TO DO WITH...

...you guessed it, chemicals. Chemicals, which comprise most everything around you, are substances that contain any particular molecule or element. Speaking of elements, find yourself a Periodic Table of Elements; it has every known element on Earth on it! An element is the smallest substance available to us; it can't be broken down into any smaller substances! These elements can form compounds, which can form molecules, which can go on to form all of what you see around you! Chemistry studies how these bonds form and why, based on the number of electrons in the atoms and which electrons are attracted to another atom.

The concept of the atom goes all the way back to the ancient Greeks. Democritus was the first person to believe that matter could be broken down into a single particle and, over time, this theory began to prove true. We've built on that theory, as we now know that atoms have a positively charged nucleus with negatively charged electrons surrounding it. The electrons are everything in chemistry, as they're what make the bonds happen!

This section is going to show you how to become a true mad scientist. Blast off with some rockets and discover the secret to harnessing heat!

LIVELY 60S LAVA LAMP

- 1 cup water
- Empty clear water bottle
- Funnel
- Vegetable oil
- Food coloring
- Alka seltzer

GRADES: 6TH AND UP

1

Using the funnel, pour the water and the vegetable oil into the empty water bottle. Let sit for five minutes, or until the water and oil have separated completely.

What's Happening

Water is slightly polarized because of the way the hydrogen atoms (the H part of H2O) attaches to the oxygen atom (the O part of H2O). So, it has one positive side and one negative side. Oil has no charge and is

Find those 60s vibes using some ingredients from your medicine cabinet!

2 Add twelve drops of food coloring into the bottle.

3 Drop half of an Alka Seltzer tablet into the bottle.

Add ½ tablet of Alka Seltzer

Watch the magic!

4 Watch as it transforms into a lava lamp!

Science Concept: Density and Polarity

therefore non-polar. Nonpolar and polar molecules cannot mix properly, so they stay separated in the bottle.

When you drop the tablet in, it dissolves and forms a gas. The gas rises and brings with it some of the colored water. When it reaches the top, the gas escapes the water and the water sinks back to the bottom!

GLOW IN THE DARK MESSAGES

You need this

- Lemon
- Small bowl
- ¼ teaspoon water
- Cotton swab
- Sheet of paper
- Warm light source

1 Juice a lemon into a small bowl and add the water. Mix well.

2 Dip a clean cotton swab into the mixture and write a message on your piece of paper.

3 Hold the paper up to a warm light. Watch as your message becomes visible!

GRADES: 4TH AND UP

 Science Concept: Quantum Mechanics

Lemon juice has a chemical reaction with the oxygen in the air when in the presence of heat, so wherever you put the lemon juice will turn brown when exposed to a lot of heat.

Write a secret message only to have it revealed using heat!

LEMONY ACID-BASE LEMONADE

YOU NEED this

- 2 lemons
- 2 teaspoons baking soda
- 2 empty glasses
- Knife

*PARENTAL SUPERVISION NEEDED

GRADES: 6TH AND UP

Roll lemons on counter

1 Roll the 2 lemons on the countertop so that they are soft and juicy. Using your knife, cut each lemon in half and squeeze the juice into the first empty glass.

Squeeze juice into glass

2 Add the baking soda to the second empty glass.

66

Watch the lemons and the baking soda combine to form an acid-base reaction!

Pour juice into glass of baking soda and stir.

3

Pour all of the juices from the first glass into the glass with baking soda in it.

4

Stir and see what happens!

Science Concept: Acids and Bases

The lemon juice is the acid and the baking soda is the base! This reaction creates CO_2 (in the form of bubbles), which are released when the reaction happens.

ACID? BASE?
RED CABBAGE CAN TELL YA!

Is it an acid? Is it a base? Red cabbage can indicate!

You NEED this

- Water
- Blender
- 5 leaves of red cabbage
- Strainer
- 5 glasses
- Vinegar
- Spoon
- Baking soda

GRADES: 7TH AND UP

1 Pour water into a blender until it's halfway full and add five red cabbage leaves. Blend on high until the mixture is almost completely a liquid.

2 Strain the mixture evenly into five separate glasses. Set one glass aside as a control.

3 Pour a little bit of vinegar into one of the four remaining glasses and stir. Vinegar is acidic, so the liquid should react by turning pink. You can use this to gauge how acidic other substances are.

4 Repeat step three with baking soda in a separate glass. Baking soda is basic, so the liquid should react by turning green. You can use this to gauge how basic other substances are.

5 You can repeat steps three and four with any number of substances, including lemon juice, hand sanitizer, shampoo, etc.

Science Concept: Acids and Bases

Acids and bases are tested using the pH scale. Bases have a very high pH while acids have a very low pH. The pH scale ranges from 0-14, with 7 being considered neutral (water is a neutral substance). You can determine whether a substance is an acid or base using an indicator, which will change color based on the pH level of a substance. Purple cabbage juice is considered an indicator because it has anthocyanin (a pigment that changes color based on pH level). So, red cabbage can tell you if something is an acid or a base!

SCIENTIST PROFILE
AQUATIC TOXICOLOGIST

Debbie Desjardins is an Aquatic Toxicologist at a Contract Research Organization (CRO), where she tests and evaluates the impact of agrochemicals on aquatic plants.

HOW DID YOU GET INTERESTED IN SCIENCE?

As a young child, my father was very outdoorsy and that really captured my interest in biology and ecology. **I loved the environment, seeing how everything kind of works together.** As I grew up, I think the enthusiasm of my science teachers really encouraged my interest and kept me engaged.

WHAT DID YOU STUDY IN COLLEGE?

I studied environmental science, with a focus on marine ecology and minor in chemistry and biology.

WHAT DREW YOU TO ENVIRONMENTAL TESTING?

What really drew me to being a study director and aquatic biologist was knowing that, **in my own way, I was contributing to the environment.** I get to test products and make sure they don't adversely affect the environment, and the work also combines my interest in biology and chemistry. I really enjoy crunching numbers and doing statistical evaluations of data sets that I collect, which are then presented to federal agencies to show whether or not a product should be on the market.

WHAT'S ONE OF THE MOST EXCITING PROJECTS YOU'VE WORKED ON?

One of the most exciting projects I've ever worked on was when I studied a compound used in herbicides, although I can't tell you what it was! Since the 1970s, different groups had been constantly trying to provide data to show that these compounds should be removed from the market, believing it was bad for the environment.

I did an algae study to support our research, which showed that even though the compound was toxic to the algae, it recovered 100% as soon as the compound was removed - there were no lasting effects. That study was eventually published, **which was a really big deal.**

WHAT EXCITES YOU ABOUT THE FUTURE OF YOUR FIELD?

What excites me about the testing we do is that it is always evolving; testing requirements and regulations always change based on what we learn. Over the years, society's attitude towards the environment has really changed for the better. **We are much more interested in using good strong science** to make sure that the products we use are safe for people and the planet.

MAGNIFICENT MENTOS GRAVITY GEYSER

- Diet cola soda
- Piece of paper
- Sleeve of Mentos

1 Before you do anything else, take your materials and move them outside, as conducting this experiment indoors will lead to quite a mess!

2 Remove the cap from the cola bottle. Roll up a piece of paper and cover one side with your hand. Pour the sleeve of Mentos into the roll of paper so that your hand is keeping them from falling out.

3 When you're ready, pour the Mentos into the bottle of cola. Watch as it fountains!

GRADES: 4TH AND UP

What's Happening

Soda is full of carbonation, meaning it has a lot of CO_2 in it (this is what makes it bubbly). If you ever hear someone say it sounds "flat" it's because the soda is old and the CO_2 has dissipated from the soda). When you drop something into a carbonated

Defy gravity with this Mentos and cola geyser!

Science Concepts: Chemical Reaction, Energy Release

beverage, the CO_2 rushes to surround the object. When the Mentos are dropped into the soda bottle, all of the CO_2 rushes to surround the candy. The candy, being heavy, also sinks to the bottom of the soda, so with all of that CO_2 rushing to surround the candy the CO_2 has to be released, making it rush to the top and out of the bottle!

IT'S GOLD, IT'S SILVER, NO! IT'S BRONZE!

You NEED this

- Brass key
- Soap
- Water
- Glass
- Vinegar
- 1 teaspoon salt
- Piece of copper
- Wire strippers
- 2 pieces copper wire, both 15 inches long
- 9 volt battery

PARENTAL SUPERVISION NEEDED

GRADES: 8TH AND UP

1

Clean the brass key with some soap and water. Fill a glass with vinegar and 1 teaspoon of salt. Stir well.

2

Use your wire strippers to strip the ends off of two pieces of fifteen-inch-long copper wire. Wrap one end of a wire (wire A) around the piece of copper. Hang the piece of copper over the edge of the glass, making sure it's touching the vinegar. Connect the other end of that copper wire (the end not in the vinegar) to the positive terminal of the battery.

Tightly wrap a clean brass key with copper wire

Also wrap a piece of copper with the end of the other wire

Turn a normal key into a copper key using some electricity from a battery!

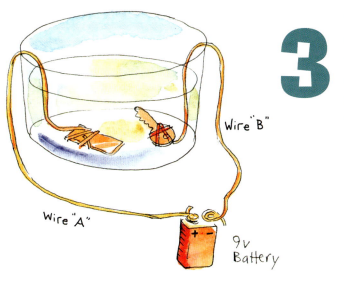

3 Take your other piece of copper wire and connect one end of it to the negative terminal of the battery. Wrap the other end of that piece around the key. Add the key to the vinegar.

4 Let sit for an hour and see what happens!

Science Concept: Chemical Reaction

The key becomes copper colored, while the piece of copper becomes brittle and breakable. When the current passes through the copper, the copper loses electrons that ionized in the vinegar. The electrons then combine with the positively charged key and the copper ions become copper atoms. These copper atoms then attach to the key and the key gets coated in a copper layering!

RAINBOW COLORED FLAMES

- Four glasses
- Water
- 1 teaspoon copper sulfate
- 1 teaspoon strontium chloride
- 1 teaspoon boric acid
- 1 teaspoon sodium chloride
- Four spoons
- Matches
- Tall candle
- 4 cotton swabs

GRADES: 8TH AND UP

1 Fill each of the four glasses with water. Add one of each chemical to their own respective glass and stir them well, each with their own spoon. We don't want any cross contamination!

STIR! (each with its own spoon!)

2 Light the tall candle.

Discover the phenomena of electrons releasing light when burned in a candle!

3

Dip a clean cotton swab into the copper sulfate glass and put into the flame, which should react by turning green. Be careful!

Dip cotton ball into each solution

Hold each one over the flame. Watch how the colors change!!!

4

Repeat step three with each of the chemicals!

What's Happening   Science Concept: Metals

The electrons of the atoms in the chemicals get excited when exposed to heat, causing them to jump to a higher energy level. When the electrons lose this energy, they emit photons (light), the color of which is determined by the energy of those electrons. Because each compound has a specific amount of energy, each will have a different color!

LIAR, LIAR, MONEY ON FIRE!

You NEED this

- Glass
- ¼ cup water
- 1 cup rubbing alcohol
- Spoon
- Dollar bill
- Fire proof gloves
- Tongs
- Lighter
- Safety Glasses

GRADES: 8TH AND UP

1
In a glass, mix together the water and rubbing alcohol. Stir well.

2
Immerse your dollar in the mixture. Put on your gloves before removing the dollar with your tongs. Light the dollar on fire and watch what happens!

 Science Concept: Liquid Properties

The water and alcohol mixture here is the key! When you light the dollar bill on fire, it burns the rubbing alcohol, which in turn heats the water and causes it to boil and evaporate. Because the bill is covered in water, the bill never gets too hot so it never catches on fire.

Burn money and spend it after!

RUBBER BONES

- Drumstick bone, cleaned
- Glass jar
- Vinegar

Eat chicken off the bone!

1 Find a drumstick bone, and make sure it's clean. If not, eat the chicken right off the bone!

Make sure it's picked <u>clean</u>

Science Concept: Chemical Reactions

The chicken bone has calcium in it, just like yours! The calcium makes the bone hard and difficult to bend. Vinegar, as we have seen plenty in this book, is an acid. The acid dissolves the calcium in the chicken bone and all the stuff that makes it difficult to bend goes away!

GRADES: 4TH AND UP

All you need is a little bit of vinegar to turn bones into rubber!

2

Place the bone in your glass jar and fill with vinegar. Seal the lid.

3

Set aside for three to seven days.

4

Open the jar, drain the vinegar, and remove the bone. Try bending it!

THE PERIODIC TABLE OF THE ELEMENTS

These elements make up everything on our planet. You probably recognize the name of some of them, but there are 118 different elements in the world! Each element gets an atomic number based on how many protons and electrons they have in their atoms.

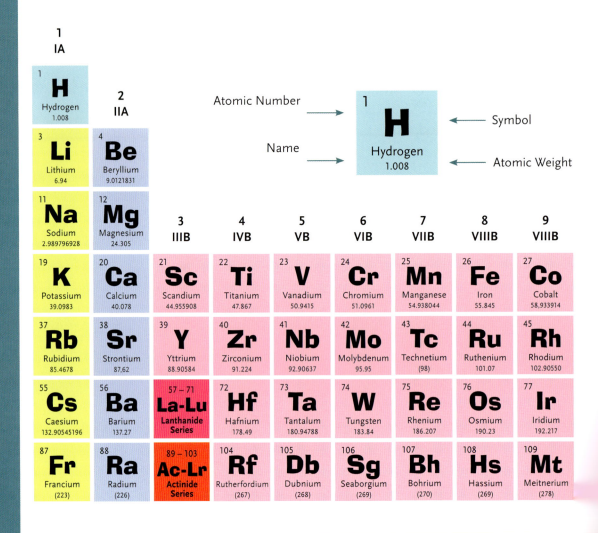

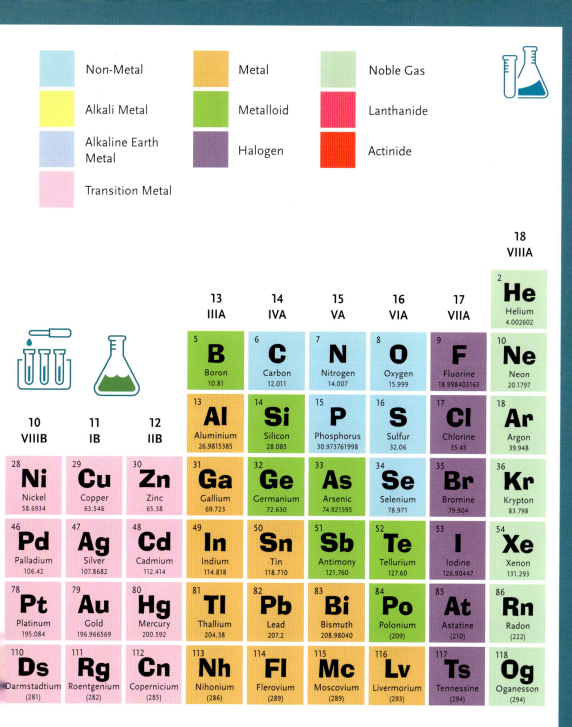

GREEN EGGS AND HAM

Pull a Dr. Seuss and eat some green eggs!

- Water
- Pot
- Stovetop
- Knife
- ½ red cabbage head
- 2 eggs
- 2 bowls
- Spoon
- Frying pan

1 Bring water to a boil in a pot over medium heat. Using your knife, cut the red cabbage into rough chunks and add to the pot. Let boil for five to ten minutes. The water should turn a deep violet color.

2 Crack the eggs into one of your bowls and remove the yolks, adding them to the other bowl. Strain the cabbage water into the bowl with the egg whites in it, which should turn said egg whites green!

3 Pour the egg whites into a medium-size frying pan and cook over medium heat. Add the egg yolks to the middle of the egg whites. Once they're cooked, go ahead and eat them!

GRADES: 7TH AND UP

Science Concept: pH and Base

Red cabbage is an indicator, as seen in the "Acid? Base? Red Cabbage Can Tell Ya!" experiment! When the red cabbage juice comes in contact with a base, it turns green, just like with the egg whites!

NO COOKING, COOKED EGG*

Cook an egg with the stove off and with no pan!

* **Egg**
* **Bowl**
* **70% rubbing alcohol**

GRADES: 4TH AND UP

* **Do NOT Eat. This experiment is NOT edible!**

Crack your egg into the bowl, making sure that the yolk stays intact. Pour the rubbing alcohol over the egg so that it is completely immersed.

Let the mixture sit for twenty minutes and watch as the egg whites turn opaque!

Science Concept: Chemical Reactions

When you cook an egg normally, the egg whites undergo a chemical reaction causing them to cook and turn opaque. Here, the rubbing alcohol is doing that. When the rubbing alcohol comes in contact with the protein in the egg white, it cooks the egg!

DENSITY ONE BY ONE

Layer some liquids based on their density and see how they stack up against one another!

- Five plastic containers
- Water
- Corn syrup
- Honey
- Dish soap
- Vegetable oil
- Food coloring
- Turkey baster
- Tall clear glass

GRADES:
5TH AND UP

1
Add equal amounts water, corn syrup, honey, dish soap, and vegetable oil to their own respective plastic containers. Add different colors of food coloring to the corn syrup and vegetable oil.

2
Use the turkey baster to start layering the liquids in your clear glass, doing so as follows: start with the honey, followed by the corn syrup, dish soap, water, and finally the vegetable oil. Be sure to clean your turkey baster between transferring each liquid.

SCIENCE CONCEPT: Density

Each layer has a different density, which is defined as mass divided by volume. In this experiment, the lower layers are denser while the top layers are less dense. Since each of the layers have about the same volume (or space that they take up), you can learn about their masses. Since the bottom layers are denser, you know that their mass must be higher than the top layers!

INSTANTLY ICY

Turn water into ice in seconds!

- At least 2 water bottles
- Freezer
- Ice cube
- Bowl

GRADES: 4TH AND UP

1 Lay your water bottles on their sides in the freezer. After about two hours, remove one of the bottles.

2 Slam the bottom of the bottle on a stable, flat surface. The contents of the bottle should turn to ice! If nothing happens, put the bottle back in the freezer for another thirty minutes.

3 Remove another water bottle from the freezer, this time pouring the contents of the bottle over an ice cube in a bowl. The water should harden into ice!

SCIENCE CONCEPT: Freezing Point

The water here is at its freezing point. The freezing point is where the water can be both a liquid or a solid. When water freezes, crystals form and gradually you get a water bottle full of them. Here, the water hasn't formed the crystals yet, so when you pour the water over the ice cube it starts to crystalize and form ice! When you slam the bottle on the table, it forms ice because it speeds up the crystallization process!

EGG GEODES

Turn an egg into a fancy, shiny geode to display around your house!

- Pushpin
- Egg
- Paintbrush
- Glue
- Alum powder
- Boiling water
- Food coloring
- Bowl
- Spoon

1 Using the pushpin, poke a hole into the bottom of the egg. Drain the egg.

2 Crack the egg shell in half. Use the paint brush to brush the glue on the inside of the shell and sprinkle the alum powder on top. Let sit overnight.

3 The next day, mix two cups of boiling water and forty drops of food coloring in a bowl. Add ¾ cup alum powder and stir to dissolve. Let cool for thirty minutes.

4 Add the eggshells to the bowl and let sit overnight. Remove the eggshells with a spoon the next day.

GRADES: 8TH AND UP

Science Concept: Chemical Reactions

The alum powder gets dissolved in the water due to the heat. When the mixture cools, the alum powder precipitates (turns back into a solid) and falls to the bottom of the bowl, onto the eggshell, and begins to crystallize and attach to the alum powder already on the eggshell.

GEODES 101

WHAT IS A GEODE?
Geodes are hollow rocks that might look plain on the outside, but are actually lined with crystals! Nodules are rocks that are much like geodes, but are completely filled with crystals, leaving no hollow.

HOW ARE GEODES FORMED?
Geodes take millions of years to form, and can occur in both sedimentary and igneous rock. They begin as bubbles in volcanic rock or hollows in the soil, like animal burrows.

Over many, many years, dissolved minerals trickle into the hollow, forming a 'shell' around the outside and slowly forming crystals along the wall of the hollow. The size, color, and shape of the crystals depends on the type of mineral, but quartz is the most common.

WHERE ARE GEODES FOUND?
Geodes can be found all over the world, and are particularly common in deserts and areas rich in limestone or volcanic ash. There are lots of geode collecting sites across the United States, including California, Utah, Indiana, Kentucky, Missouri, Nevada, New Jersey, Arizona, New Mexico, Ohio, Oregon, Illinois, Texas and the Geode State Park in Iowa.

HOW TO IDENTIFY A GEODE
Remember, geodes have to be cracked open (by a grown-up!) to reveal the crystals inside. The only way to really know you've found a geode is to see what's inside, but look out for round-ish rocks with a bumpy, uneven surface. Because they are hollow, they might also feel lighter than other rocks of the same size, and rattle a little if you gently shake them.

COLORFUL CRAYONS

- Oven
- Cookie sheet
- Wax paper
- 30 crayons
- Cheese grater
- Large bowl
- Knife

GRADES: 7TH AND UP

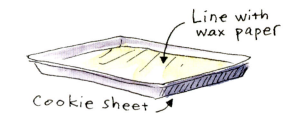

1 Preheat your oven to 200 degrees F. Line your cookie sheet with wax paper. Set aside.

Grate 20-30 crayons into a bowl. Mix colors or separate. YOUR CHOICE!!

2 Remove the wrappers from thirty or so crayons and grate them into a large bowl.

 Science Concept: Dye

When you heat the wax, it melts and then sticks to the wax next to it. If you watched the crayon shavings melt, you would notice that the darker colored crayons melt faster than the lighter colored crayons. This is because heat gets absorbed differently based on the color. Black and darker colors absorb heat faster because they're unable to reflect the light as well as lighter colors can.

Learn how to form new crayons.
Create your very own color and name it after yourself!

Fill the cookie sheet

3

Add the shavings to the cookie sheet, being sure to pack them flat so that they're between ¼ and ½ an inch thick.

4

Place the pan in the oven for fifteen minutes, or until the shavings have melted completely.

Put in oven for 10-15 min.

cut into strips

5

Remove the cookie sheet from the oven and let cool. Once cool, use a knife to cut into thin rectangular strips. These are your new crayons!

Look! I made my own crayon!

PLAYDOUGH

Ever wondered how to make playdough? Now you know! Make your very own and store it for up to 8 weeks!

You need this

- 1 ½ cup water
- Pinch of salt
- Wooden spoon
- Medium pot
- Stovetop
- 1 ½ cup flour
- 3 teaspoons cream of tartar
- Food coloring

1 Add the water and salt to a medium pot and stir until the salt is dissolved. Turn the burner on medium heat.

2 Stir in the flour, cream of tartar and your choice of food coloring. Stir continuously. When the edges of the mixture begin to pull away from the sides of the pot, remove the pot from the burner.

3 Once cooled, knead the dough until it achieves the consistency that you desire. If you store the dough in an airtight plastic container it should last for about two months!

Science Concept: Mixing

Although this is a little less science based, playdough can actually conduct electricity! Stick the end of an LED into one end of a ball of playdough and a wire connected on one end to a battery in the other. Stick another wire into the ball of playdough and then onto the other terminal of the battery. The LED will light up! This is because of the salt in the playdough, which is made up of elements that you can conduct and pass electricity through!

GRADES: 8TH AND UP

MARVELOUS MILK ART

Make your own Jackson Pollock painting using a different medium: milk and food coloring!

- Milk
- Plate
- Food coloring
- Liquid soap
- Cotton swab

GRADES: 4TH AND UP

1 Pour some milk onto a plate and let settle completely. Add a few drops of food coloring to the center of the plate.

2 Place some liquid soap on the end of the cotton swab. Set the end down in the food coloring and let sit for fifteen seconds.

3 See what happens to the milk!

Science Concept: Surface Tension

The milk and the soap are both nonpolar molecules. The water that holds the milk molecule in it, however, is polar, meaning it has a charge to the particle. When you add the soap to the milk, the soap combines with the nonpolar molecule and dissolves it. The fatty polar molecule in milk then separates and moves the milk!

SKI HANDS
Feel the heat with this homemade hand warmer!

- 1 tablespoon iron fillings
- 2 tablespoons calcium chloride
- Sandwich bag
- 2 tablespoons warm water

GRADES: 4TH AND UP

1
Mix the iron fillings and calcium chloride together in a sandwich bag.

2
Add the water to the bag and mix well. Feel the heat!

Science Concept: Stored Chemical Energy

The energy for this reaction comes from the iron filings. When the air and the iron mix, the iron rusts and creates heat. The salt simply accelerates the reaction and creates more heat!

CAN YOU STEEL THE HEAT?

Use a chemical reaction to steal the heat from steel wool and vinegar.

- 2 cups vinegar
- 2 clear glasses
- Steel wool
- Sheet of paper

GRADES: 4TH AND UP

1 Pour the vinegar into the clear glass. Soak the steel wool in the vinegar for eight minutes.

2 Remove the steel wool from the vinegar and squeeze the excess out over the glass. Place the steel wool in the second clear glass.

3 Place the piece of paper over the top of the glass. Watch the heat escape!

Science Concept: Chemical Reactions

When you soak the steel wool in vinegar, the outer protective layer of the steel wool dissolves. This means that the steel will now rust in the presence of air in a chemical reaction. So, when you put the steel wool into the glass and put the piece of paper on top, it will trap the heat caused by the reaction and create steam, causing the wool to rust!

HAND HEATING SLIME

You Need This

- 2 tablespoons thermochromic pigment
- Food coloring
- 2 bowls
- 8-ounces Elmer's glue
- Water
- 1 teaspoon borax

*PARENTAL SUPERVISION NEEDED

GRADES: 7TH AND UP

1 Determine the color of your thermochromic pigment and select a food coloring different from the pigment.

2 In a bowl, mix together the Elmer's glue and ¼ cup water. Add a few drops of food coloring and stir. Repeat with the Thermochromic pigment.

3 In a separate bowl, mix together the borax and ¼ cup water. Stir well before adding the mixture to the first bowl. Stir well.

4 Knead the mixture until it achieves your desired consistency. The more you knead it, the less slimy it will be!

See how your hands can change this slime's color!

 What's Happening Science Concept: Heat Transfer

The thermochromic pigment is what changes the slime color due to heat. This kind of pigment is designed to change color at a specific temperature. So, when you go beyond the normal temperature of the slime, it will change color in response!

PLASTIC MILK

- 3 tablespoons vinegar
- 1 cup hot milk
- Bowl
- Spoon
- Paper towel

*PARENTAL SUPERVISION NEEDED

GRADES:
4TH AND UP

1 Pour the vinegar into the bowl.

2 Heat the milk on the stove.

3 Pour the hot milk into the bowl with the vinegar and mix well.

Pour milk into vinegar

Make a model of whatever you want by turning milk into plastic.

4

Once it solidifies, put the milk curds on a paper towel.

put "curds" onto a paper towel

5

knead it together

Knead all of the curds together. Make sure to get rid of any excess water using the paper towels.

6

You can now mold your milk into any shape!

Sculpt away!

What's Happening Science Concept: Chemical Reactions

Vinegar is, surprise, a mild acid and thus can change the pH level of given mixtures. When it is added to the milk, the milk's molecular makeup begins to break apart and form new molecular chains. This is what happens when the milk curdles. This causes the plastic like substance that you can mold into whatever shape you want.

POCKET VOLCANO

- Foam modeling clay
- Tall glass
- 2 tablespoons baking soda
- ½ cup vinegar

1

Mold the foam modeling clay around the tall glass to make it look like a volcano. Bring the glass outside and set in an open area.

2

Put the baking soda into the "volcano." Add the vinegar and watch as the mixture explodes!

GRADES: 4TH AND UP

 Science Concept: Acid-base Reaction

Vinegar is a weak acid and baking soda is a base. When acids and bases react, or get mixed together, they form an acid-base reaction. This forms carbonic acid, which breaks apart into carbon dioxide and water with a bunch of energy. That extra energy has nowhere to go but up, so it explodes out the top!

Make your ingredients go

KABOOM

in your very own volcano-style chemical reaction.

ELEPHANT TOOTHPASTE

- Goggles
- Gloves
- ½ cup 40 volume hydrogen peroxide
- Dish soap
- Food coloring
- Tall glass
- 4 tablespoons warm water
- 1 package dry yeast
- Spoon

*PARENTAL SUPERVISION NEEDED

GRADES: 7TH AND UP

1 Put on your goggles and gloves. You're going to want to do this experiment outside so that you don't make a mess!

2 Add the hydrogen peroxide to your empty bottle, followed by a squirt of dish soap and fifteen drops of food coloring. Set aside.

Create an explosion with hydrogen peroxide, because who doesn't want another explosion!?

3 In your glass, mix together the warm water and package of dry yeast. Stir well.

4 Pour the yeast mixture into the bottle and watch it foam!

 Science Concept: Chemical Energy

The yeast acts as a catalyst for the hydrogen peroxide, helping to break it down into H2O (water) and O2 (oxygen). When the yeast mixture mixes with the peroxide, it begins to break down and the oxygen gets released in the form of bubbles, creating the foam!

CO₂ BUBBLES

Instead of making bubbles with air, make bubbles with dry ice! Watch them fill with CO_2 gas, and pop then to see a puff of homemade smoke!

- Exacto knife
- 2 plastic cups
- Bowl
- Warm water
- Soap
- Gloves
- Dry ice

1 Use the exacto knife to cut the bottom out of one of the plastic cups. Set aside.

2 In your bowl, mix together the water and soap until the mixture is very bubbly. Set aside.

3 Put on your gloves! Add your dry ice and warm water to the second cup and set aside.

4 Dip the top of your first cup into the soapy mixture so that it forms a seal across the top. Now, gently set it bottom first into the cup with the dry ice. Watch as a bubble forms over the top!

Science Concept: Sublimation

Dry ice sublimates, meaning it goes straight from a solid to a gas at room temperature. The dry ice turns to a gas and pushes against the soapy top, forming a bubble!

*PARENTAL SUPERVISION NEEDED

GRADES: 8TH AND UP

PEEP
THE MARSHMALLOW

Make a marshmallow three times its original size just by exposing it to some heat!

- Paper towel
- Microwave
- Marshmallow

*PARENTAL SUPERVISION NEEDED

GRADES: 5TH AND UP

1
Place a paper towel down in your microwave and set the marshmallow on top.

2
Close the microwave and set to one minute. Watch as the marshmallow expands!

Science Concept: Chemical Bonds

The reason the marshmallow expands is because of the chemical bonds in the marshmallow. When you turn the microwave on, the water molecules begin to heat up. This creates steam, which makes the marshmallow get bigger. Once the steam leaves the marshmallow you have only sugar left over. So, as it continues to heat, the marshmallow turns brown because the sugar gets so hot that it breaks down and caramelizes.

SHAKE IT LIKE A SLUSHY

No blender? No problem!
All you need is a freezing point to make this slushy!

- 1 cup fruit juice
- 2 quart-size bags
- 2 tablespoons rock salt
- Ice

GRADES: 4TH AND UP

1
Add a cup of fruit juice to one of the quart-size bags, seal shut, and place inside of the other quart-size bag.

2
Add the rock salt and ice to the space remaining in the outermost quart-size bag and seal it shut.

3
Shake the bags for five to ten minutes, or until the juice is frozen and slushy. Once the desired slushiness level is achieved, take it out and eat it!

Science Concept: Freezing Point

Shaking the bag causes the temperature of the ice to lower the temperature of juice in the inner baggie. This causes some of the juice to freeze, resulting in a slushy!

WHAT IS MATTER?

Matter is everywhere and everything, from the air you breathe to the book you're reading. All matter is made up of tiny particles called atoms, which are so small they can't even be seen through an average microscope!

By definition, matter is anything that has mass and takes up space (mass is a combination of the type and density of atoms in something, and the total number of atoms in it) and can be found in 3 major states: solid, liquid, or gas.

These states are determined by how tightly a substance's atoms are packed together. The term used to describe this is density. The higher the density, the tighter the atoms are packed.

SOLIDS

Solid matter is made up of atoms that are packed tightly together—so tightly that you can't push or move through it. It will also hold its shape at room temperature and only change shape under force (like being broken or cut). Think of a brick wall, a wooden floor, or small objects like a hammer, a phone, or a pair of diceHowever, even in solids there is a tiny space between each atom, and some solids are denser than others. For example, most metals are denser than plastic or wood. This means that there is less space between the atoms of the metals than the atoms of plastic or wood.

LIQUIDS

Like solids, liquids will always take up the same amount of space - this means that solids and liquids have a definite volume. Yet unlike solids, liquids won't retain their shape at room temperature. Instead, they take on the shape of whatever container they are in, whether that's a bottle or a bath tub. This is because there is more space between the atoms of a liquid, allowing each atom to move around more. That's why you're able to stick your hand under water or swim across a pool, while you can't simply walk through a wall!

GAS

We are constantly surrounded by gases, even though we are able to move through them without even noticing. Gases (including the air we breathe) are made up of atoms that are barely touching one another, always moving, and will expand to fill whatever space they are in. If you were to pop a balloon, the air compressed inside would immediately expand to fill the entire room! This is because gases are are not as affected by gravity as solids or liquids.

STATES OF MATTER

CAN'T YOU BELIEVE IT'S BUTTER?!

Enjoy your very own butter! Don't forget to add the toast!

- 1/3 cup heavy cream
- Pinch of salt
- Small jar with lid

1 Add the heavy cream and a pinch of salt to the small jar and seal shut.

2 Shake the jar for fifteen to twenty minutes, or until the heavy cream turns solid.

GRADES: 4TH AND UP

Science Concept: Chemical Bonds

Heavy cream has a lot of fat in it, which is why it is thicker than milk. When you shake the bottle, the particles of fat stick together and turn into butter. The salt is only added for taste! You can make butter without the salt, but it doesn't taste as good!

POP POP POWDERED SHERBET

Sherbet goes pop, pop, pop! Make some delicious popping sherbet and share it with your friends!

- 2 teaspoons citric acid
- 1 ½ teaspoons tartaric, ground
- 1 cup powdered sugar
- 3 tablespoons Kool-Aid mix
- 2 teaspoons baking soda
- Plastic bag

GRADES: 6TH AND UP

1
Put the citric acid, tartaric, powdered sugar, Kool-Aid mix, and baking soda into a plastic bag.

2
Seal shut and shake well. Serve and enjoy!

SCIENCE CONCEPT: Chemical Reactions

Just like the volcano, an acid-base reaction is happening here. The baking soda is the base and the citric acid is the acid, which forms CO_2 bubbles when mixed together! This releases and causes the popping sensation!

EDIBLE GLASS

Design your own window and turn sugar into glass!

- Butter or shortening
- Pan
- Large pot
- Pinch of cream of tartar
- 1 cup white sugar
- ¼ cup corn syrup
- ½ cup water
- Food coloring

1

Grease your pan and set aside. In your large pot, combine the cream of tartar, sugar, corn syrup and water. Bring to a boil over medium-high heat.

2

Let the water boil for about one minute before carefully pouring into the prepared pan. Add some food coloring to the mixture and mix it around a little bit. Let cool before removing the "glass" from the pan! Be sure to be careful when you eat your experiment since, like real glass, this edible glass can be sharp!

GRADES: 8TH AND UP

Science Concepts: Heat, Solid

Normal glass is made by heating sand. This process is similar but involves sugar instead. Once the mixture cools, it turns into an amorphous solid, or a solid with a disorganized structure.

PEANUT BUTTER POLES

Make gum disappear with nothing but peanut butter!

- 1 piece of gum
- Spoon
- Creamy peanut butter

1 Place a piece of gum in your mouth and chew for about one minute.

2 Take a spoonful of creamy peanut butter and add to your mouth. Notice what happens to the gum as you chew!

GRADES: 4TH AND UP

Science Concept: Nonpolar Molecules

Gum and peanut butter are both nonpolar. This means that the molecules that make up peanut butter and gum are not polarized and therefore are neutral molecules. Nonpolar molecules can dissolve other nonpolar molecules. When you chew the gum and peanut butter, the chewiness of the gum starts to go away and eventually the gum dissolves due to its nonpolar properties.

ICE CREAM IN A BAG

- 1 cup half & half
- 2 tablespoons white sugar
- 1 teaspoon vanilla extract
- 2 quart-size bags
- 2 gallon-size bags
- 5 cups ice
- ½ cup rock salt
- Gloves

GRADES: 6TH AND UP

1 Mix together your half & half, sugar, and vanilla extract in one of the quart-size bags.

2 Push all of the air out of the bag before sealing shut. Make sure there are no air bubbles!

3 Add the sealed bag to another quart-size bag and seal shut. Add these bags to one of the gallon-size bags.

 ## What's Happening

The rock salt lowers the temperature of the ice to below 0 degrees Celsius! Lowering the freezing point means that the ice can cause the milk to freeze. When you shake the bag, the small baggie on the inside moves around and, as a result, the cold temperature

Ice cream in a bag! It's as easy as milk, sugar, and salt!

4 Add five cups of ice and ½ cup of rock salt to the bag and seal shut. Add to another gallon-size bag and seal shut. The extra bags are meant to prevent leaking!

Shake for 15-20 minutes

Ice, Rock Salt

1 gallon bag

5 Put on your gloves. Shake the bags for about fifteen minutes, or until the contents of the innermost bag are frozen.

Mmmmm!

6 Remove and enjoy!

Science Concept: Condensation and Physical Reactions

lso transfers to the mixture nside. This makes the ice cream old! Similarly, just like in an't You Believe its Butter?!" e fat particles in the milk or half & half get smashed together due to the shaking, causing some solidification.

111

ROCK N ROLL CANDY

- Cup of water
- Pot
- Stovetop
- Granulated sugar
- Scissors
- Skewers
- Jar
- Food coloring
- Clothespin

GRADES: 7TH AND UP

1 Add the cup of water to the pot and bring to a boil. Slowly stir in your sugar, doing so until it will no longer dissolve in the water. Remove from heat and allow the mixture to cool.

2 Cut the tips off of the skewers. Rinse them underwater and roll them around in two and a half cups worth of granulated sugar. Let dry.

Rock around the candy clock and after a few days enjoy your edible rock candy!

3

Pour the sugar mixture into your jar and add any food coloring of your choice. Place the skewer into the jar, suspending it at the top with your clothespin. You don't want the skewer touching the bottom of the jar!

4

Place the jar in the refrigerator for about a week before enjoying your rock candy!

 What's Happening Science Concept: Phase Changes

The water can hold a lot more sugar when it's heated than it can when it's not. As the sugar mixture begins to cool, the water can no longer hold that large amount of sugar and it begins to precipitate, meaning it turns back into a solid. The sugar from the water begins to stick to the sugar of the coated skewer, forms a crystal, and creates rock candy!

WHO'S WHO IN

Marie Curie

Arguably one of the most famous women in science, Marie Curie was a Polish chemist and physicist. She is the only person to ever win the Nobel Prize in two different categories: chemistry and physics. After moving to Paris to continue her education, she met her future husband, Pierre. They partnered up to study radioactive properties, for which they won a Nobel Physics prize in 1905. After her husband passed away in an accident, she won the Nobel Chemistry prize in 1911 for the discovery of polonium and radium. The work Marie Curie contributed to involved a lot of radiation, which is very dangerous in large doses. She later passed away from complications due to long exposure to radiation. In fact, her notes are kept in a vault because they are still radioactive.

Stephanie Kwolek

Stephanie Kwolek helped to develop a series of materials that were synthetic, most notably Kevlar. Born in the U.S., she received a Bachelors degree from Carnegie Mellon but never went on to get her doctorate degree. She worked at DuPont, a chemical company, and it where she discovered the strong and important properties of the materials she was working with. Kevlar is what makes up a bullet proof vest and is five times stronger than steel. Her work continues to benefit us today, as our knowledge of polymer materials really starts with her!

CHECK OUT THIS PERSON!

CHEMISTRY

Dmitri Mendeleev

Author of a defining work in chemistry titled *Principles of Chemistry*, Mendeleev is considered one of the co-creators of the periodic table of elements. Having found a pattern in chemical properties that he was trying to classify, Mendeleev had a dream where "all elements fell into place as required." He woke up and wrote everything down as he had dreamt it, the result of which was a nine-element periodic table of elements that Mendeleev began expanding from there. The result was an early iteration of the classroom staple that we all know today.

Linus Pauling

One of just two people to ever win Nobel Prizes in different fields, Linus Pauling joined the company of Marie Curie thanks to his work with DNA structures and, more importantly, his founding the fields of quantum chemistry and molecular biology. Having published over 1,200 works, Pauling worked on everything from the nature of a chemical bond to molecular genetics to structures within the atomic nucleus.

Humphry Davy

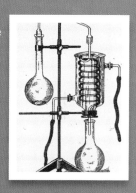

Davy, who passed away in 1829 at age 50, accomplished quite a bit during his time as a chemist: he isolated a series of substances for the first time, starting with potassium and sodium and expanding to calcium, strontium, barium and boron, he discovered the elemental nature of both chlorine and iodine, and he invented the field of electrochemistry. He also invented an early version of the incandescent light bulb, part of an invention that he called the "Davy Lamp." Though not totally correct, his theory on acid-base reactions that he came up with in 1815 served as the popular thought for the remainder of that century.

PHYSICS

Isaac Newton was a British physicist, mathematician, and all around genius who single-handedly started modern physics and developed the math required to do so. He is most famous for his Laws of Motion, which we'll be touching on a lot in this section. These laws are the basis for physics and describe the way we interact with objects every day. The first law states that an object at rest will stay at rest, or that an object in motion will stay in motion unless acted on by a force. The second law can be broken down into the equation $F=ma$, or force equals mass times acceleration. The third law states that all forces are equal and opposite.

That all may seem like a bunch of mumbo-jumbo, but you interact with these laws every single day! A stationary ball won't move unless you push it and it won't stop until the air creates a drag on it. In a game of pool, hitting the 8-ball with the cue ball will cause it to move away from me, in accordance with Newton's second law, and not toward me, which would be in violation of Newton's third law!

Another man to whom the field of physics owes a great deal is Albert Einstein. Einstein was extremely smart and dedicated his life to thinking about gravity, doing so in terms of light. He believed that the speed of light was constant, a belief that served as the basis for his General Theory of Relativity, which states that objects with large masses bend the space around them. In other words, gravity bends space!

Here, you will discover a whole new world of scientific concepts; they might seem like magic, but most can be explained away using Newton's laws or the theory of electromagnetism.

GRAVITY BENDS SPACE!

FOREVER WET SAND

Make your own kinetic sand. Play with it to relieve stress and add some fun to your day!

- Oven
- 2 cups sand
- Cookie sheet
- Bowl
- 2 teaspoons dimethicone

GRADES: 7TH AND UP

1
Preheat the oven to 225° F. Place the sand on a cookie sheet and let bake for two hours.

2
Remove the cooking sheet from the oven and let cool. Pour the sand into your bowl and add the dimethicone. Mix until the sand starts to stick together. If it doesn't, you might need to add another ½ teaspoon of dimethicone to the mixture!

3
Play with the sand!

Science Concept: Kinetics

Adding the dimethicone makes the sand stick together, making it easier to play with and mold into different shapes!

OUT WITH THE OLD PAPER, IN WITH THE NEW!

Make new paper out of old paper strips. Crumple up that old test that's been collecting dust and give it new life!

You Need This

- Newspaper
- Blender
- Water
- Window screen
- Plastic tub
- 2 towels

PARENTAL SUPERVISION NEEDED

GRADES: 6TH AND UP

1
Tear the newspaper into several large strips and add to the blender. Add enough water to cover the paper. Blend the water to a pulp, adding more water if necessary.

2
Set the window screen over the plastic tub. Pour the contents of the blender over the screen. Put the towel over the pulp and press down, getting as much water out of the paper as possible. Don't break the screen!

3
Once all of the water has been drained from the paper, place a new towel over the screen and flip onto a flat surface. Remove the screen and let the paper air dry for one to two days.

Science Concept: Physical Mixing

Paper is made from trees and cellulose fibers. These cellulose fibers, when wet, are easy to combine to form even more paper!

OOEY-GOOEY SLIME

Green slime can be made at home! Form both a solid and a liquid and have fun messing with it!

- Bowl
- Cornstarch
- Water
- Food coloring

GRADES: 4TH AND UP

1 Add one cup of cornstarch and ½ cup of water to a bowl and mix together with your hands.

2 You want your slime to have the consistency of honey, though it's really a matter of preference. Keep adding cornstarch and water until your desired consistency is achieved!

3 Add a few drops of food coloring and enjoy your slime!

Science Concept: Non-Newtonian Fluids

The slime is a non-Newtonian fluid. Non-Newtonian fluids act both like solids and like liquids. The slime here can be molded into a solid but also behaves like a liquid. You can see this when you play with it. This is because the cornstarch is not fully dissolved, as the molecules are suspended in the water. Neat, huh!

WATER RISE

Make the water rise in a cup with some matches!

- Plate
- Water
- Food coloring
- Candle
- Lighter
- Glass cup that is both taller and wider than your candle

GRADES: 7TH AND UP

1

Fill your plate with water and add some food coloring. Place the candle onto the middle of the plate and light it.

2

Place the glass upside down over the candle. Watch as the water level rises in the cup.

Science Concept: Air Pressure

When the candle burns, it burns up oxygen in the air. These oxygen molecules take up a lot of space, so when they get burned off there is less stuff on the inside of the glass. Having less stuff in the glass puts less pressure on the water directly under the cup, compared to outside the cup where there is more pressure on the water. This difference in pressure outside the cup pushes the water higher into the cup!

DANCING SLIME

- Speaker *
- Plastic wrap
- Slime made in the Ooey-Gooey Slime experiment
- Source of music

Ask a parent before using

GRADES:
4TH AND UP

1 Lay a speaker down on its back so that it's facing up.

2 Cover the entire face of the speaker with plastic wrap.

 What's Happening

See what happens during low pitches versus high pitches. Low pitch means that the frequency of the sound wave is lower (low frequency means larger amplitude), where high pitch means the frequency

122

Slime is the next big dance move.
Make the slime dance using a sound system!

3

Place your slime from the previous experiment over the plastic.

Watch slime move when speaker plays low and high frequencies!

4

Play some music through the speaker and watch what happens to the slime!

Science Concept: Sound Waves

her (high frequency means smaller e amplitude). The low pitches pen less often (less frequent) so the e has a lot of time to "jump" before the next pitch (or wave) comes. The high pitches happen very quickly (more frequent) so the slime has less time to "jump!"

SUPER SPINNING CANDLE

- Long candle
- Knife
- Needle
- Two identical glasses
- Matches

GRADES:
7TH AND UP

1

Make sure that the wick is exposed at both ends of the candle. If it isn't, use the knife to cut off an inch of the covered side at a time until the wick is exposed.

2

Push the needle through the middle of the candle so that it sticks out of both sides evenly. Let the needle rest on the outer rims of the two glasses, which should support the candle.

3

Light both ends of the candle and watch it swing back and forth!

See how a candle will teeter and totter back and forth due to its change in weight.

 Science Concept: Newton's Laws

The candle spins because of Newton's forces! The candle wants these forces to be balanced, so the heavier part of the candle dips and, as a result, burns the wax off of its side to lose mass and weight. Once it weighs less than the top of the candle, the candle will swing so that the original top part becomes the bottom part. This repeats until the candle is completely burned through!

A FORK, A SPOON AND A TOOTHPICK WALK INTO A YOGA CLASS

Learn about an object's center of mass and the forces that act on it!

You need this

- Fork, the cheaper the better
- Spoon
- Toothpick
- Tall glass

GRADES: 5TH AND UP

1

Push the two center prongs of the fork upward a little bit. Push the spoon under those two prongs so that it's over the two outer prongs.

2

Push your toothpick through the gap between the two center prongs. Carefully set the toothpick on the rim of the glass so that the face of the fork and spoon are facing the glass. You might have to slide it across the rim to find the best balance point!

Science Concept: Newton's Forces

The main force that we're working with in this experiment is gravity, which acts on all of the objects. We then have a tension force acting from the toothpick onto the fork, the spoon, and the glass. When these forces act on each and are balanced, the utensils will stay in place!

FEVERISHLY FLOATING ORANGE

Does the orange peel make an object sink? Float? Find out with this experiment!

- Sheet of paper
- Pencil
- A glass wide enough to fit an unpeeled orange
- Orange

GRADES: 4TH AND UP

1
On a sheet of paper, write down whether or not you think that an unpeeled orange will float in water. What about a peeled orange?

2
Fill the glass with water and set the unpeeled orange in it. Remove the orange, peel it, and repeat. Did the results of the experiment support what you wrote down?

Science Concept: Buoyancy

The orange has gravity acting on it, so gravity is pushing it down. However, thanks to Newton's laws, the water is also pushing back against the orange (equal and opposite, right?!). When the water's "pushing" force is equal to the force of the gravity, an object floats and is buoyant. Here, the unpeeled orange floats because the peel has air pockets that bring in air and displaces the water.

TOTALLY TUBULAR VELOCITY

How do magnetism and electricity work to create motion? Use a magnet to find out.

- A long copper piping that will fit your magnet
- Magnet

GRADES: 4TH AND UP

1 Hold the tube upright, vertical to the ground.

2 Place the magnet into the top of the tube.

3 See what happens as you let it go!

Science Concept: Lenz's Law

This is another version of Maxwell's Laws. Maxwell's Laws are a series of electro-magnetic laws that combine both electrodynamics and magnetism. In fact, they form the very basis on which the concepts of classical optics, magnetism, and electrical circuits are built!

UP AND AROUND THE MAGNET

Chart the magnetic field lines of a magnet, the same way sailors do for the Earth!

- Sheet of white paper
- Magnet
- Compasses
- Pencil

GRADES: 5TH AND UP

1
Set your sheet of paper down on a flat surface and place your magnet in the center.

2
Set your compasses anywhere around the magnet. They should all be pointing toward the same thing; draw a line from the compass to where it's pointing to. Do this for all of your compasses.

Science Concept: Magnetic Fields

Magnets create a magnetic field. This magnetic field can be charted using a compass, as a compass has a mini magnet in the center. When subjected to an external magnetic field, the compass will align with the magnetic field, which you can chart and "see" using your pencil. This is very similar to how the Earth works. The Earth's core creates a magnetic field, which defines what north and south are. We can then follow it using a compass and see where we are!

TABLE TOP SPIN

Magnets can create motion through a change in field. Visualize it with a heart shaped wire!

- Copper wire, 8 inches
- AA battery

GRADES: 7TH AND UP

1 Bend your copper wire so that it's in the shape of a heart, with the two ends meeting at the bottom. Stand your battery up so that the negative side is resting on a flat surface.

2 Bend the ends of the copper wire 90 degrees in opposite directions away from the face of the heart shaped wire. In other words, if you're looking at the wire with the heart shape facing you, one of the wire ends should be pointed directly at you while the other is pointed directly away from you.

3 Set the dip of the heart directly over the positive terminal of the battery. Let the inside of each wire end hug the exterior of the battery (but not too tightly); they should be about one centimeter above the negative terminal.

4 Watch as the wire spins around!

Science Concept: Induction

The battery creates a magnetic field due to Maxwell's laws, which state that a current carrying wire will create a magnetic field. So, the battery creates a current through the wire, which induces a magnetic field, which acts on the wire and causes it to rotate!

MAGNETIC FLUID

Iron is intrinsically magnetic.
See how this makes one cool fluid!

- Gloves
- Mask
- 1 tablespoon iron oxide
- Vegetable oil
- Small jar
- Test tube
- Magnet

1

Put on your gloves and mask. Add one tablespoon of iron oxide and ¼ cup vegetable oil to a small jar and mix well, being sure to mix out any clumps.

2

Add one teaspoon of vegetable oil and two drops of the iron oxide mixture to the test tube. Put a magnet against the outside of the test tube so that it's right next to the iron oxide. Move the magnet around the outside of the test tube and the iron oxide should move with it!

GRADES: 8TH AND UP

Science Concept: Magnetic Field

Iron oxide is magnetic because iron, along with a few other metals, has magnetic properties. When you move the magnet around the iron oxide will move with it because it is attracted to the metal. This type of magnetic fluid is called ferrofluid, which behaves like a liquid but is responsive to an external magnetic field.

CRUSH A CAN WITHOUT THE HULK!

- Ice water
- Spoon
- Aluminum can, clean
- Pan
- Stovetop
- Small bowl
- Tongs

GRADES: 7TH AND UP

1 Add three spoonfuls of water to the can.

Add water to the clean can

2 Set the can in the pan and place over medium heat and let alone for a minute or two. Add ice water to a small bowl until it is about an inch deep.

← Ice water

132

Use pressure to crush a can with the same ease that the Hulk would have!

3 Once the can has steam coming out of it, remove it from the pan with tongs and quickly flip it upside down into the ice bowl.

Watch the can collapse!

4 The can should crush onto itself!

What's Happening   Science Concept: Air Pressure

When the can is on the stove, the air pressure inside the can decreases because it loses the air and water that was originally inside of it. Boiling the can turns the water inside of the can to vapor, pushing out all of the air molecules. Flipping the can over forms a seal, resulting in the air pressure inside of the can being lower than the air pressure outside of the can. This difference in pressures causes the can to collapse!

EGG IN A BOTTLE

Suck an egg through the neck of a bottle using pressure and volume.

- Glass bottle
- Vegetable oil
- Hardboiled egg, shell removed
- Bowl of water
- Sheet of paper
- Lighter

1 Grease the top of the glass bottle with vegetable oil. Dip the egg into the bowl of water and place the smaller end into the top of the bottle.

GRADES: 7TH AND UP

2 Fold a piece of paper together lengthwise and set the tip of it on fire. Remove the egg from the bottle, place the piece of the paper into the bottle, and set the egg back down. Watch as it slides through the top!

 Science Concepts: Thermodynamics and Boyle's Law

re, it is all about air pressure. When you put the burning piece of paper in e bottle and put the egg on top, the air inside the bottle gets hot and begins expand. This expanded air wants to escape (like when you blow up a balloon o much and it pops), forcing the egg to vibrate. When the piece of paper stops ing, the air inside the bottle cools and, as a result, takes up less space. The pressure on top of the egg is therefore greater than the air pressure inside ottle, so we have uneven forces (again, Newton). The egg then slides into the bottle because the air pushes it in!

BOTTLE BALLOON

- Water bottle
- Balloon, 8-10 inches
- Rubber band
- Water
- Hammer
- Nail

GRADES; 6TH AND UP

1

Remove the cap from your water bottle. Place the balloon inside of the bottle so that that part that you would normally use to inflate it is in the mouth of the bottle. Open that part up and wrap it around the mouth of the bottle. Secure with a rubber band. Now try to inflate the balloon. You'll notice that you can't.

2

Remove the balloon from the water bottle. Fill the bottle with water and put the cap back on. Use the hammer and nail to puncture a hole in the bottle about an inch and a half from the bottom.

3

Empty the water and remove the cap. Repeat step one. You'll notice that the balloon inflates this time!

 Science Concepts: Pressure, Molecules

The reason you couldn't blow up the balloon the first time was because the air in the water bottle already took up all of the space. When you added the hole, there is a way for air to escape in order to allow the balloon to grow. So, when you blow the balloon up the air is pushed out of the hole in the side.

Fill a water bottle with a balloon using gas properties!

HOW MUCH WATER CAN LINCOLN HOLD?

- Penny
- Dropper
- Water

GRADES: 4TH AND UP

1 Place the penny on a level surface.

2 Fill your dropper with water and start placing droplets onto it.

3 Count how many drops of water that the penny can hold before it spills over the edge!

 What's Happening

Water molecules, made of one hydrogen atom and two oxygen atoms, are polarized, meaning they have a positive charge on the top and a negative charge on the bottom. This means that each water molecule is attracted to another, linking the positive end to the negative end of another molecule and so on until you have a chain. This attraction is called cohesion. The molecules at the surface do not have

How much area does a penny have? How much water does that correspond to? The result may surprise you!

Science Concept: Surface Tension

any other molecules attached to them, so they are more strongly associated to the water molecules next to them. This creates a film on the surface of the water, called surface tension. When you add enough water, the cohesive forces, the forces that hold together all the water and create the surface tension, break under the force of gravity, causing the water to spill over the edge. Surface tension is how some insects travel over water in ponds or lakes. The surface tension is so strong that it can hold the weight of the bug!

JELL-O IN THE DARK

Ever wanted to make Jell-o at night?! Now you can!

1
Pour one cup of tonic water into the pot. Bring to a boil.

Bring to boil

- Tonic water
- Pot
- Stovetop
- Package of Jell-O mixture
- Large bowl
- Spoon
- Clear glasses
- Black light

2
Pour the package of Jell-O into a large bowl.

3
Mix in the boiling water and stir until all of the crystals have dissolved.

Stir until crystals are dissolved

GRADES: 7TH AND UP

6 Place in the fridge for four to five hours.

4 Add one cup of cold tonic water to the bowl and stir.

Glasses will glow!

5 Add the Jell-O mixture to several clear glasses.

7 Remove the glasses from the fridge. Shine the black light on them and watch them glow!

 What's Happening Science Concept: Light

The black light shows light that emits in the ultraviolet. UV has a higher frequency than visual light and also has a higher energy. The reason you don't see things glow fluorescent is that in order to see something glow you have to have enough energy to excite the atoms. Normally lights don't have enough energy for UV, but a black light does! Here, the tonic water contains quinine, which is a fluorescent substance that glows under a black light. So, when you shine a black light on it, it glows!

CHLADNI PLATES

- Bluetooth speaker
- Bowl
- Parchment paper
- Rubber band
- 2 tablespoons colored sand
- Smartphone *

* Ask a parent before using

GRADES:
4TH AND UP

 Science Concepts: Frequency, Nodes

When you play the different tunes, the parchment paper will vibrate based on its resonance frequency. Resonance is the natural frequency that a specific object will vibrate at and each object has a few resonant frequencies. As you travel through different frequency ranges, the patterns will change. The reason that this experiment is called Chladni plates is because Ernst Chladni was a famous physicist who discovered that plates could vibrate at a resonant frequency.

See what kind of patterns that different tunes make on parchment paper!

1

Turn the Bluetooth speaker on and place it in the bowl. Cover the bowl with a sheet of parchment paper and secure to the mouth with a rubber band.

2

Put the sand over the parchment paper. Play a song over the Bluetooth speaker, making sure that it's loud, and watch what happens to the sand!

SIMPLE CIRCUITRY

Build an electrical circuit using a piece of wood and a light bulb!

YOU NEED this

- 2 3-inch pieces of copper wire, ends stripped
- 6 V battery
- Electrical tape
- Plank
- Metal thumb tack
- Light bulb
- Clothespin
- Piece of wood

PARENTAL SUPERVISION NEEDED

GRADES: 8TH AND UP

1

Tape an end of one of the copper wire pieces to the negative terminal of the battery using electrical tape. Set the battery down on the piece of wood. Use a metal thumb tack to secure the other end of the wire to the wood.

2

Wrap one end of the other piece of copper wire around the metal base of the light bulb once. Secure the wire in place using a clothespin, being sure to keep the base of the light bulb exposed. Tape the other end of the copper wire to the positive terminal of the battery.

3

Grab the light bulb by the clothespin and maneuver it so that the base is touching the top of the thumb tack. The light bulb should light up!

Science Concept: Electricity

The battery is the power source for the circuit and the copper wires allow the energy to flow. Connecting the light bulb and metal thumb tack completes the circuit!

LEMON-LIME POWER

See how a lemon can power a small circuit with ease!

- 2 pennies
- Soap
- Water
- Scissors
- Tin foil
- Ruler
- Lemon
- Knife
- Paper clips

GRADES: 7TH AND UP

1 Clean the pennies with soap and water. Set aside.

2 Cut a sheet of tin foil into three strips, each about one inch wide and eight inches long. Fold each of these strips lengthwise into thirds.

3 Lay a lemon down on its side on a flat surface. Using a knife, make four cuts that are each about an inch long and half an inch deep. Add a penny to the first and third cuts. Place one of the tin foil strips into the second cut and bend it over so that it touches the penny in the third cut, using a paper clip to secure the two.

4 Secure another tin foil strip to the penny in the first cut with another paper clip. Add the final piece of foil into the fourth cut in the lemon.

5 Bend the tops of the tin foil strips in the first and fourth cuts toward each other so that they're about one centimeter apart. You should feel a tingling sensation, which is the electricity!

Science Concepts: Electricity, Acid

The tingling sensation is electricity! The two electrodes here are the copper penny and the aluminum foil while the electrolyte is the lemon juice.

SCIENTIST PROFILE
MICROBIOLOGY LECTURER

Davida Margolin is a lecturer at the University of New Hampshire, where she teaches over 500 students a semester all about the world of germs.

DO YOU REMEMBER YOUR FIRST SCIENCE PROJECT OR EXPERIMENT?

Absolutely, second grade Science Fair. My friend and I went down to Woolworths and bought a mouse. Our fathers built a maze with us out of wood, and we trained that mouse to run through the maze and jump over toothpicks.

WHAT DREW YOU TO THE FIELD THAT YOU'RE IN?

I loved animals and biology and really wanted to be a vet, but in high school I was told I shouldn't bother since veterinary schools were unlikely to accept a girl. I ended up going down a whole different path, and worked in photojournalism and graphics for many years. Eventually I realized that I owed it to myself to pursue my dreams, and I enrolled back in college. I took all the pre-veterinary requisites, but the microbiology classes I took just blew me away, so I wound up focusing on that. I still think I'm a veterinarian, but my patients are just really small!

HOW DID YOU BECOME A LECTURER?

I went back to school for my Master's, and one year they didn't have anyone to teach a class I was assisting with, Germs 101. I volunteered and have been teaching it ever since! Whether they are bacterial, viral, or parasites, germs are absolutely fascinating. It's one of UNH's largest classes, and designed to engage non-science majors.

WHAT IS YOUR FAVORITE PART OF YOUR JOB?

Interacting with the students, in any way shape or form, even when they are being ridiculous. I love listening to the stuff that they are thinking about. I'm very lucky—in a big class students are often too intimidated to speak, but mine are happy to.

WHAT MAKES YOUR JOB IMPORTANT?

My students leave my class with a better understanding of the world around them and how things relate to one another, which is absolutely imperative. By teaching my students about germs and diseases, I teach them things they need to know in life to protect themselves and their families.

WHAT ADVICE WOULD YOU GIVE TO POTENTIAL FUTURE SCIENTISTS?

Talk to your teachers, read everything you can about the topics that interested you (making sure any website you visit is fact-based). If you have an interest in anything, follow it through and don't let anyone squash your dreams.

WHAT EXCITES YOU ABOUT THE FUTURE OF YOUR FIELD?

I'm excited about technological innovation, and find anything from a medical perspective fascinating, whether it's testing viruses to preventing cancer. Honestly, if you go into a career in microbiology or public health you will never be bored!

EXPANDING SLIPPERY SOAP

Turn soap into a new shape with nothing but a microwave. Don't forget: the soap is still perfectly good to use!

- Bowl
- Water
- Bar of Ivory soap
- Knife
- Microwaveable plate
  Paper towel
- Microwave

GRADES: 7TH AND UP

1
Fill the bowl with some water and add the bar of Ivory soap. Notice whether it floats or sinks. Remove the soap from the bowl and, using the knife, slice in half. You'll see that it's solid, not hollow! Slice your halves in half again.

2
Cover your microwaveable plate with a paper towel and place two of the soap quarters on top. Microwave the soap for two minutes. Let the soap cool completely and observe the new shape!

Science Concept: Heat Expansion

The ivory soap is solid, but is less dense than water. When you cut the bar of soap, you can see some smaller air pockets. When you heat the soap, the air pockets expand, causing the soap to take on a new shape. This is caused by Charles's Law, which states that as a gas is heated, its volume will expand! Charles's Law is based on the ideal gas law, written as $PV = nRT$. P is pressure, V is volume, n is the number of moles (6.02×10^{23} molecules) of a substance, R is a constant that helps both sides of the equation equal each other, and T is temperature. As you can see, if you increase T, nRT all begins to increase, so since $PV = nRT$, so should PV. So if pressure stays the same, this means that V should increase!

MAGNETIC TRAIN

You Need This

- Copper wire
- AA battery
- Ruler
- Wire cutters
- 6 neodymium magnets

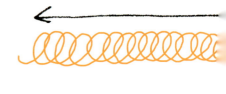

1

The first step here is to create three feet of coiled wire that will act as the tracks for your train. So, take the uncut wire and wrap it around your battery, doing so until you have your three feet of coiled copper wire. Use the wire cutters to cut the coil from the rest of the wire.

Watch the battery move down the tube

GRADES: 7TH AND UP

💡 **Science Concepts:** Magnetic Fields, Inducta

Electromagnetism is guided by Maxwell's Laws, one of which states that a changing electric field will create a magnetic field. Placing the battery into the copper coil created an electric field, which in turn created electric current in the copper. This current then moves the battery "train" through the coil!

Batteries create currents, which in turn create magnetic fields. See this in action as the battery travels through the coil with ease!

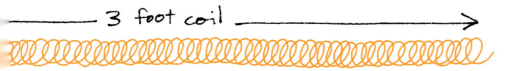

2 Add three magnets to each end of your battery.

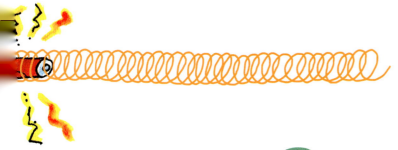

3 Put your train in the end of the coil and watch it travel through unassisted!

EARL GREY READY ROCKET

- Scissors
- Tea bag
- Plate
- Matches

1 Use the scissors to cut off the top of the tea bag. Empty the tea from the bag and either discard or save for future consumption.

Cut off the top of a teabag and empty out the tea.

2 Turn the teabag upside down and place it on to the plate, so that it can stand up on its own.

teabag
Plate

GRADES: 7TH AND UP

 What's Happening

As the tea bag begins to burn, the temperature of the air inside of it begins to climb higher than the temperature of the air outside of it. Hot air increases in volume and, here, that volume has nowhere to go except out the bottom of the bag.

You can transform a small tea bag into a rocket in three, two, one, blast off!

Light teabag

Teabag will float off as it burns.

No one has ever been able to do this!

3 Light what is now the top of the tea bag on fire using the matches. Now step back and watch as the ash begins to float away!

Science Concepts: Air Expansion, Currents

Hot air also rises, so when the tea bag fills with hot air it begins to float as a result of the increased volume and the temperature difference between the inside and the outside of the bag. When the tea bag finally burns all the way through, the ash will become light enough for the convection current created by the heat to make it take off!

POP CORN ON THE COB

- Popcorn on the cob
- Microwave-safe bag
- Microwave

GRADES: 5TH AND UP

 What's Happening

When the microwave distributes heat throughout the popcorn, the water in the popcorn kernels begins to heat up. When the water gets hot in the popcorn kernel, the water expands. When it gets too hot

Pop popcorn off of the cob using heat!

1 Place the popcorn on the cob into the microwave-safe bag. Fold the top of the bag down several times.

2 Place the bag in the microwave and cook for three minutes. Remove the bag and let cool. Enjoy your snack, observing how the popcorn comes off of the cob!

Science Concept: Heat Expansion

and the water gets too big, the kernel pops! This is another variation of the ideal gas law, Charles's Law. Charles's Law states that as temperature increases, volume of a gas increases. When the water turns to a gas inside the kernel, the volume gets bigger, which causes the pressure to increase and it pops!

TORNADO TWISTER TANGLE

- 2 empty 2-liter soda bottles
- Water
- 3 tablespoons glitter
- Washer
- Duct tape

GRADES: 4TH AND UP

1

Fill one of the soda bottles with water until it's about ¾ full. Add three tablespoons of glitter. Fasten the washer to the top of the bottle.

2

Place the other bottle upside down on top of the washer. Secure the mouths of the bottles together with duct tape.

Form your own tornado vortex with water and glitter!

Flip over and spin for a few seconds

3
Turn the bottles upside down and move in a circular motion for a few seconds.

Watch the tornado!

4
You should see a tornado start to form! If it doesn't work at first, don't worry! It might take a few tries until you get the motion right.

 Science Concept: Centripetal Force

When you turn the bottle system upside down and start to spin it, t creates a centripetal force. The water forms a vortex due to the forces and the spinning, which looks like a tornado!

BUCKET SWING

- Bucket
- Water

1 Fill the bucket halfway to the top with water.

2 Grab the handle of the bucket and spin the water in a circle.

NOT SURE THIS WILL END WELL!

3 Slowly turn the bucket upside down, continuing to spin while doing so. Notice that the water doesn't fall out of the bucket!

GRADES: 4TH AND UP

Determine how centripetal force acts on water in a bucket!

 What's Happening   Science Concept: Gravity

When you spin the bucket, gravity is still acting on it; however, the spinning of the bucket causes something called the centripetal force. This force is dependent on velocity, or speed (velocity is speed with a direction). When you spin the bucket, if the speed with which you spin the bucket is going faster than the speed at which gravity is pulling down on the water, the water will not fall out! Try this (be prepared to get wet!): spin the bucket fast and start to slow it down. You'll notice that the water will begin to fall out!

FREEZING WIRE

You NEED this

- Sponge
- Ice cube
- Fishing wire
- 2 12-ounce soda bottles, full
- Ruler
- Gallon jug filled with water

1 Place the sponge on a flat surface. Set an ice cube on top of the sponge.

2 Tie each end of the fishing wire to the tops of each soda bottle.

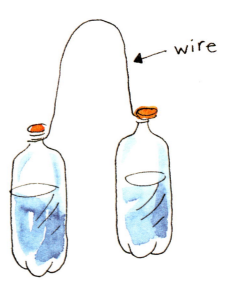

GRADES: 6TH AND UP

Cut ice and refreeze it using nothing but fishing wire.

3 Set your ruler down so that half of it rests on a flat surface and the other half sticks off of that flat surface. Use the rock to secure the ruler.

Hang the bottles on either side so the wire **presses** down on the ice cube.

4 Place the sponge and the ice on the end of the ruler that is sticking off of the flat surface. Place the middle of the fishing wire across the top of the ice cube. Watch as the ice melts and then freezes again as the wire goes through the cube!

 Science Concept: Pressure and Temperature

When you try to cut the ice cube with the wire, the pressure increases the temperature on the ice and causes the ice to melt. This makes the wire go through the ice cube. The water then gets cold again (due to the ice around it) and it refreezes.

WALKING ON EGG SHELLS

- 4 dozen large eggs, with packaging

Ask a parent before using

1 Make sure all of your eggs are fully intact. Align all of the eggs so that the pointier end of each egg is facing down.

GRADES: 5TH AND UP

 Science Concept: Dispersed Pressure

The shape of the eggs makes them very strong, as they evenly distribute the pressure caused by your feet when you walk on them.

Walk along a bunch of eggs without breaking them!

2 Line up two cartons side by side. Place the other two cartons side by side in front of the first two. Try walking across them!

Lay out cartons of eggs to make a "path"

3 Without any shoes on, have a friend help you step on one of the dozens of eggs. Walk along the eggs!

WALK ON EGGS!

SLING SHOT CATAPULT

- 10 popsicle sticks
- 4 rubber bands
- Glue
- Water bottle cap
- Raisin

GRADES:
6TH AND UP

1

Stack eight popsicle sticks on top of each other. Rubber band both ends of the stack so that it is secure.

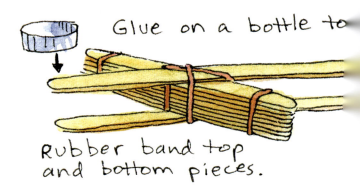

2

Place one popsicle stick on top of the stack and one popsicle stick underneath the stack so that they're parallel with each other and perpendicular with the rest of the stack. Secure these two new popsicle sticks together using another rubber band, crossing it so that an X forms over the part of each popsicle that meets the original stack.

 What's Happening

When you load the raisin into the bottle cap and bend the popsicle stick back, that popsicle stick then has potential energy, or energy that has the potential to be converted into movement. When you

Have a competition with your friends to see who can send their raisin the farthest!

3

Pinch one end of the two popsicle sticks together and secure with another rubber band. Glue your water bottle cap so that the top is facing down on the opposite side of the popsicle. Let dry.

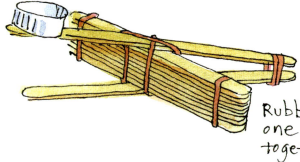

Rubber band one end together.

Load up a raisin and "Fire Away!"

4

Your catapult should be ready to go! Put your raisin inside of the cap, push down, and release!

Science Concept: Trajectory

release the popsicle stick and the raisin goes flying, that potential energy gets transferred to kinetic energy, which is energy being used for movement. This process represents the conservation of energy!

FREE FALLING EGG

Drop an egg. Will it smash? Up to you!

- Cardboard box
- Egg
- Padding (toilet paper, bread, toothpicks, blankets, etc.)

1

This is a design your own experiment! The objective is to pad the box enough so that you can drop an egg into it without having it break. Consider turning this into a design competition with your friends!

2

It's up to you!

GRADES: 4TH AND UP

Science Concepts: Gravity, Forces

This is all about physics! When you drop the egg from the second floor, gravity accelerates the egg toward the ground. If you drop the egg from high enough, the egg and box will reach terminal velocity, which is the fastest speed an object can reach while falling through air. When the egg hits the ground, the momentum of the egg gets transferred to both the ground and the rest of the objects in the box or in your set up!

RUBE GOLDBERG ACTIVITY

Use conservation of energy to make a ball travel due to many reactions!

- A ball
- You decide the rest!

1
This is another design your own experiment! A Rube Goldberg experiment is one in which one reaction causes a series of reactions. Grab a bunch of moving parts and get started!

2
Make it as small or as large scale as you want!

GRADES: 4TH AND UP

Science Concept: Conservation of Momentum

Rube Goldberg is based around the idea of conservation of momentum. Conservation of momentum is the idea that the initial momentum and the final momentum are equal. Momentum is defined as the mass multiplied by the velocity (remember, velocity is speed with a direction). For example, if a ball hits the dominoes, its velocity and thus its momentum is transferred (i.e. conserved) to the domino, which is turn transfers its momentum!

MR. POTATO CLOCK

You need this

- 2 potatoes
- 2 short nails
- 2 short, heavy copper pieces
- 1 V LED clock
- 3 alligator clips with wire units

GRADES: 8TH AND UP

1
Set one of your potatoes on its side. Insert your nail on one end and your piece of copper on the other. Do the same with the other potato.

2
Remove the battery from the 1 V LED clock. Connect one side of an alligator clip to the positive terminal in the clock's battery compartment and the other side to the copper piece in the first potato.

3
Connect one side of another alligator clip to the negative terminal in the clock's battery compartment and the other side to the nail in the second potato.

4
Connect one side of the last alligator clip to the nail in the first potato and the other side to the piece of copper in the second potato.

Why buy batteries when you can use potatoes to power your clock!

 Set your clock and watch it keep time!

💡 Science Concept: Electrical Circuitry

Here, the chemical energy of the potatoes is transferred to electrical energy. The copper piece and the zinc in the nail react within the potato, transferring the electrons to the wires and creating a current, which flows to and powers the clock!

BALLOON VROOM VROOM

You need this

- Hammer and nail
- Water bottle
- 3 straws
- Glue
- Scissors
- 4 large water bottle caps
- 2 skewers
- Balloon
- Tape

GRADES: 8TH AND UP

1

Using the hammer and nail, puncture a hole straight through both sides of the water bottle about an inch from its base.

2

Do the same at the top. The result should be two holes on each side of the bottle.

3

Slide a straw through each set of holes and trim so that only about one inch is sticking out on either side. If the holes are too big to secure the straw, glue it in place.

Make a car that only needs some air to move along the ground.

4 Use the hammer and nail to make a hole in the center of each water bottle cap. Feed a skewer through the cap so that its top is facing out. Glue in place.

5 Slide the skewer through one of the straws. We want the cap to be pretty close to the water bottle. Once the cap is about an inch away from the bottle, let sit. Slide another water bottle cap through the skewer on the other side so that it too is about an inch from the bottle. Glue in place and trim off the excess skewer. Repeat for the other skewer.

6 Tape the balloon along the length of the third straw so that it can still be inflated. Then glue the straw on top of the car so that the mouth of the balloon faces the same direction as the back of the car.

7 Blow your balloon up and watch the car go!

Science Concepts: Momentum and Drag

Newton's Third Law states that every reaction has an equal and opposite reaction. So, the air in the balloon becomes potential energy, and when you let go of the air the release of the air and energy in the balloon is translated to movement through the wheels. So here, the release of air (the initial reaction) has an equal response of the wheels!

SERIES CIRCUIT

Explore the world of electric circuits!

- Copper wire
- 2 1 V light bulbs
- Electrical tape
- 6 V battery

GRADES: 8TH AND UP

1
Wrap copper wire around the bottom of the light bulb, making sure that there are at least two inches of excess wire sticking out on both sides. Secure in place with electrical tape. Repeat for the other light bulb.

2
Tape another piece of wire, about four inches long, to one terminal of the battery. Connect it to one of the pieces of wire sticking out of the base of the light bulb. Secure with electrical tape.

3
Repeat for the other terminal and other light bulb. Connect the two remaining pieces of wire sticking out from the bases of the light bulbs and they should light up!

Science Concept: Electricity

When light bulbs are in a series, meaning they are next to each other in a circuit, they share the voltage!

PICKY PI

3.1415926.... Measure this special number using any circular object!

- Any circular object (ball, bottle, pie, etc.)
- Ruler
- Sheet of paper
- Pencil
- Tape measure

GRADES: 5TH AND UP

1
Find a circular object. It can be a ball, a bottle, or even a pie! Just as long as it has a measureable radius.

2
Measure the diameter, making sure that you do so through the center of the circle. Record this measurement. Now, using your tape measure, measure the circumference of the circle. Record this measurement too.

3
Time for some math! The circumference of a circle is equal to that circle's diameter multiplied by pi. To solve for pi, divide the circumference by the diameter. The equation should yield a value between three and four! Do this for several circular objects and compare the values that you get!

Science Concepts: Observations, Pi, Irrational Numbers

Pi is an irrational number with a never-ending range of decimals, starting with 3.14159265! It is the ratio of a circle's circumference to its diameter and it comes up frequently in math and physics. Although it seems silly, you need it when solving for the area and volume of various curved surfaces.

SOLAR S'MORES

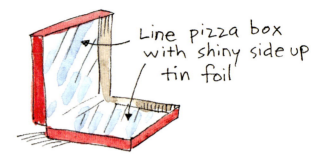

Line pizza box with shiny side up tin foil

1

Cover the inside of the pizza box with the tin foil, shiny side facing out. Use the chopstick to prop the pizza box open. Secure with tape.

- Pizza box
- Tin foil
- Chopstick
- Tape
- Graham cracker
- Chocolate
- Marshmallow

Tape a chopstick to hold the box open

2

Top a graham cracker with chocolate and marshmallow in the pizza box and set it in the sun. Make sure that the open side of the box is facing the sun; adjust the angle to get as much sun as possible.

GRADES: 4TH AND UP

The Sun produces a lot of heat. Harness it to make a s'more!

Put chocolate on marshmallow on top of graham cracker & place it facing the sun.

3

After about an hour, check on your marshmallow. Once it has cooked, enjoy!

 Science Concept: Heat

The heat from the sun gets transferred to the marshmallow by way, in part, of the tin foil; the shiny side of the tin foil reflects the light onto the marshmallow, speeding up the cooking process.

MAGNIFYING HEAT

- Piece of wood
- Magnifying glass

GRADES:
6TH AND UP

1

Lay the piece of wood down on the ground outside on a sunny day.

Magnifying glasses have another purpose besides making things larger! Put your name into a piece of wood using one.

2

Hold the magnify glass up to the sun, trying to focus the light on the piece of wood. It should start to burn!

 Science Concept: Magnification

The lens focuses the light onto the wood, intensifying it to the point that it can actually burn its surface!

CANDY CHROMATOGRAPHY

See what colors dyes are made of!

You need this:

- Coffee filter
- Plate
- Any type of colored candy
- Water
- Water dropper

1

Place the coffee filter on a plate and smooth out all of the edges. Place a pile of candy in the center, noting the type of candy and how many pieces there are on the top corner of the filter. Add five drops of water to the candy. Let sit for ten minutes. As the colors start to run, you'll be able to see which colors make up the dye of the given candy!

Science Concepts: Dye, Color

Chromatography is where you use paper to see the various components in a mixture. Each dye travels at a different speed. Dyes that can dissolve in water will travel farther while dyes that can't will travel less!

GRADES: 4TH AND UP

3D POLARIZED

Polarized light is what makes 3D glasses work!
See how you can use polarized light!

- 3D glasses with polarized lens
- Mirror

GRADES: 4TH AND UP

1
Put the glasses on and tilt your head while looking in the mirror. Notice how the lights and colors look different?

2
Pop out one of the lenses. Hold it up to the light and see how the light reacts based on the lens' orientation.

3
Pop out the other lens. Stack them on top of each other and hold them up to the light. Rotate the top lens and see what happens to the light.

Science Concept: Light Polarization

3D glasses create polarized light, which is when a light wave has a specific orientation and direction. Normally, light can travel anyway it wants, but when it passes through the lens it travels in a certain direction due to its properties. When you have the two lenses on top of each other, they go black and opaque. This is because when the light gets polarized and you add another lens on top, the already polarized light has no components that travel in other directions. So, the light cannot pass through it!

STATIC LIGHTNING

Static electricity is the name of the game. Build a charge and let it show you lightning!

YOU NEED this

- Scissors
- Garbage bag
- Tape
- Rubber gloves
- Iron pan with a plastic handle
- Iron fork

*PARENTAL SUPERVISION NEEDED

GRADES: 6TH AND UP

1
Use your scissors to cut along the sides of a garbage bag so that you can spread it flat across a table. Secure with tape.

2
Put on your rubber gloves and grab the plastic handle of your pan. Turn the lights off. Rub the pan back and forth on the table. Pick up the iron fork and bring it close to the edge of the pan. You should see a spark!

💡 Science Concept: Static Electricity

e reason you see a spark is due to static electricity. When you rub the pan on plastic it builds up charge, meaning you are picking up electrons, creating et charge. Once you have the net charge and you hold the fork close to the pan, e electrons want to neutralize with the pan, so they "jump" across and form a spark! Your body does not spark because your feet are planted firmly on the ground, meaning that you're grounded so the charge can run straight through you to the floor!

CANDY CRUSH LIGHT

- Mint Life Savers (don't get sugar-free!)
- Plastic bag
- Pliers

1

Place the Life Savers in the plastic bag and, before sealing, press all of the air out of it.

Put lifesavers into a baggie and squeeze out as much air as possible.

 Science Concept: Light

This is an example of tribo- luminescence which is where light is created due to the crushing or smashing of an object. The sugar in Life Savers has a specific structure and, when you break that structure, it rips the electrons away from it and the pieces become charged. So, the electricity jumps from one piece to another and makes a spark!

GRADES: 6TH AND UP

Discover the bright lights hidden in a Life Saver!

2

Turn off all of the lights in the room. Wait a few minutes for your eyes to adjust.

3

Use the pliers to crush the candy in the bag. Watch for the spark!

CRUSH the lifesavers and watch what happens!!!

RAINBOW THROUGH WATER

- Drinking glass
- Small mirror
- Water
- Flashlight
- Wall

GRADES: 4TH AND UP

1

Set the glass on a flat surface. Set the small mirror inside of the glass so that it is angled upwards. Fill the glass with water.

Diffraction creates a rainbow of light! Use this to see how white light can be changed to a rainbow!

2

Turn off the lights. Make sure the room is as dark as possible. Shine the flashlight onto the mirror and look at the projected rainbow!

 Science Concept: Diffraction

White light is a combination of all the colors of the rainbow. When you use the mirror (you can also use a prism) it divides the white light into its components, ROYGBIV, or red, orange, yellow, green, blue, indigo, and violet. The water refracts the light, meaning the water molecules will bend the light, so the rainbow gets "bent" after leaving the water.

CLEAR RAINBOW

Clear nail polish can create an iridescent rainbow on black paper!

- Bowl
- Water
- Clear nail polish
- Sheet of black cardstock

1

Fill your bowl with water. Add three drops of clear nail polish to the water and wait for it to disperse. Dip the sheet of black cardstock into the bowl. Remove and let dry. Rainbow patterns should form on the cardstock once dry!

GRADES: 6TH AND UP

Science Concepts: Films, Color

The paper gets coated in a thin layer of clear polish, which when held to the light shows different colors when you change the angle of the paper. This is due to the properties of the clear polish. The nail polish on the paper does not have a certain thickness, so it varies across the top. Light travels through the polish, hits the paper, and emits back out. These light waves then hit each other and form various colors!

RAINBOW REVEAL

See how colors can mix using the capillary properties of paper towels!

- 9 identical jars
- Water
- Red, yellow, and blue food colorings
- 6 paper towel sheets

GRADES: 5TH AND UP

1
Create three separate rows made up of three jars each. Fill the leftmost and rightmost jars to the tops with water.

2
In the first row, add red food coloring to the left jar and yellow food coloring to the right jar. Stir. In the second row, add yellow food coloring to the left jar and blue food coloring to the right jar. Stir. In the third row, add red food coloring to the left jar and blue food coloring to the right jar. Stir.

3
Get six paper towels and fold each in half lengthwise twice. Place one end of the paper towel in each jar containing water and fold the other end over the empty jar in the middle. Let sit for about an hour. Watch as the colors begin to mix in the middle jar!

Science Concept: Mixing

Capillary action in the paper towels brings the water from the left and right jars and adds it to the center jar. The water then mixes in the jar to form a new color!

MINI HOVERCRAFT

You need this

- Hot glue
- Water bottle pop top
- CD
- Balloon

*PARENTAL SUPERVISION NEEDED

GRADES:
5TH AND UP

1 Glue the top of the water bottle top over the center hole of the CD. Let dry.

2 Place the CD on a flat surface, making sure that the pop top is closed. Blow up the balloon and pinch the end of it shut. Wrap the mouth of the balloon over the water bottle top, making sure that no air escapes.

3 Open the pop top of the water bottle. Give the CD a nudge and it should float across your flat surface!

See how hovercrafts could work in the future by building a small-scale version!

 Science Concepts: Air Pressure, Density

When the air in the balloon escapes through the pop top, it creates an air flow between the CD and the surface of the table. This reduces the friction because it lifts the CD off of the table, so when you give it a nudge it is free to travel and hover over your flat surface!

ELECTRIC MOTOR

- 2 metal paperclips
- Electrical tape
- D battery
- Copper wire
- Ruler
- Marker
- Wire cutters
- Magnet

GRADES:
8TH AND UP

1 Grab the outermost end of each paperclip and bend it back 180 degrees so that it sticks straight out. Use the electrical tape to secure the end of the straight line that you just formed to either side of the battery. Repeat with the other paperclip on the opposite side of the battery. Do it in a way so that the faces of the paperclips are facing each other above the battery.

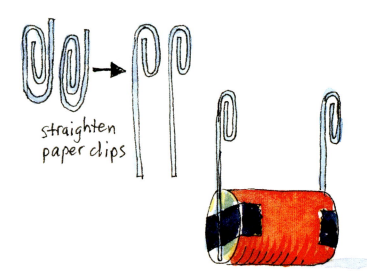

straighten paper clips

2 Take your copper wire and measure two inches from the end. Start wrapping the wire around your marker from that point, keeping the wire tight and compressed in the process. This will form the coil. Once you've wrapped the wire around the marker ten times, carefully pull the marker away from the wire. Measure two inches past the coil on the opposite side and, using your cutters, cut the wire.

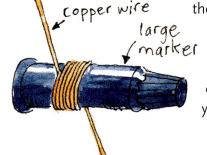

copper wire
large marker

Create a small motor using copper wire and the properties of electromagnetism!

3 Loop each end of the wire through the top of the coil that you've just created. Pull the wire through the bottom of the coil and bend it so that it faces the direction that it did at the start of this step. This ensures that the wire coil is secure.

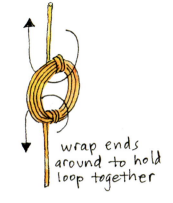

wrap ends around to hold loop together

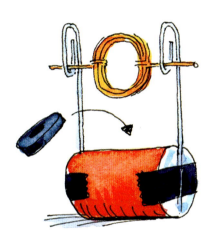

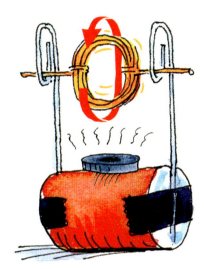

4 Laying the battery on its side, thread the ends of the copper wire through the paperclips so that they're holding it up. Place your magnet in the center of the battery. Give the coil a nudge and it should begin to spin!

 Science Concept: Electricity

The wire and the paperclips form a closed circuit. This allows a current to travel from one battery terminal to the other by way of the copper wire. The current that travels through the copper wire creates a magnetic field (thanks to Maxwell's Laws) which then interacts with the magnetic field created by the magnet that rests on the battery, causing the copper coil to spin!

BASIC BINARY NUMBERS

Determine what a binary number is and see how to solve for the binary version of any number!

- One package of candy (anything that you can count will do! Skittles work best!)
- Sheet of paper
- Pencil

GRADES: 6TH AND UP

1 Count out a number of candies, record this number on a piece of paper and circle it. Let's go with eleven pieces for the first time through the experiment.

2 Divide your candy in half. If there is any remainder, write a "one" underneath your circled number. If no remainder, write "zero." Put the remainder piece and one half of the candy into the discard pile.

3 Repeat step two with the remaining candy. If after dividing the pile in half there's a remainder, write it underneath the circled number from step one or, if applicable, the remainder number from step two.

4 Repeat these steps until you're left with one piece of candy. Write a "one" at the base of the column of numbers that you should have by the end of the experiment. Read the column from bottom to top. This is the binary number of your original number! So, if you started with eleven candies, the binary number for the number eleven is 1011.

Science Concept: Computing

Binary numbers are in base of two, which is why we kept dividing all of the candies into two groups. They're made up of bits; for example, the binary number for eleven is 1011 and contains four bits. In really easy computer codes, the code takes all of the information you have and changes them into ones and zeros. You can even put letters into binary! The computer then reads the list of binary numbers and can understand them the way that we understand 1867 or 2000001!

PICK A CARD! ANY CARD!

Use this easy card game to impress all of your friends!

- Deck of cards
- Friend

1 Shuffle the deck well. Have a friend pick any card in the deck.

2 Split the deck in half. Glance at the bottom card in the top half of the deck, making sure that your friend doesn't notice. Ask your friend to shuffle the deck.

3 Once they hand the deck back to you, flip the cards over and find the card that you glanced at in part two. Their card should be right below that one.

4 Ask them if that is their card! Sometimes this trick doesn't always work because they shuffle the deck really well. Try again and it should work!

GRADES: 6TH AND UP

Science Concepts: Patterns, Math

Here, you are working with probability. Probability is the study of the likelihood of something to occur. During this trick, you are betting on the idea that the other person probably won't shuffle very well. There is always a slight chance that it won't work out, but by doing this you are betting that there is a greater chance the person won't shuffle the deck well, so you can pick their card with no problem!

WHO'S WHO IN

Chien-Shiung Wu

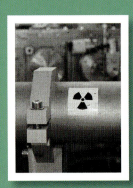

Chien-Shiung Wu was a Chinese physicist who worked mostly with nuclear physics. During World War II, she joined the Manhattan Project at Columbia University and did her research primarily on radiation detectors. She later worked with two theoretical physicists with whom she tested the law of conservation of parity during beta decay. This law states that all objects and their mirror images behave in similar ways; however, she designed an experiment, which proved that nuclear particles do not always act similarly. Although she was not given the Nobel Prize with her collaborators, she did receive tenure at Columbia University, where she helped to do work with blood and sickle cell anemia.

Niels Bohr

The founder of the Institute of Theoretical Physics at the University of Copenhagen, Bohr left his mark wherever and whenever he could throughout his life. A Danish physicist, he received the Nobel Prize in Physics in 1922 for his work in developing an understanding of the quantum theory and atomic structure, which was essential in our greater understanding of those things today. He was also responsible for creating the Bohr model of the atom, which embraced general principles and concepts that remain valid today.

Bohr fled Germany in 1943, fearing that he would be arrested for helping those fleeing Nazism, and eventually ended up in Britain. It was from there that he would assist on the Manhattan Project, which was responsible for developing the nuclear bombs that were dropped on Japan during World War II. Bohr insisted on worldwide cooperation in regards to nuclear energy after the war.

CHECK OUT THIS PERSON!

PHYSICS

Erwin Schrödinger

Schrödinger was an Austrian physicist who, like Bohr, made significant contributions in the field of quantum theory. A Nobel Prize winner himself, he developed the wave equation and formed the fundamental basis of wave mechanics, both of which serve to describe waves as they occur in physics.

Schrödinger was also a philosopher, for which he is best known for his thought-experiment "Schrödinger's cat." It was a paradox that he used to point out the problems in common thought regarding quantum mechanics, especially in regards to the way that they were being interpreted.

Ernest Rutherford

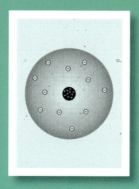

Coined by *Encyclopedia Britannica* as the greatest experimentalist since Michael Faraday, Rutherford was a British physicist who is often referred to as being the father of nuclear physics. He identified the nuclear transmutation in radioactivity, discovered the concept of radioactive half-life, and differentiated alpha and beta radiation. He was even awarded a Nobel Prize in chemistry for the work. He later developed the Rutherford model of the atom and performed an experiment that led to the first splitting of the atom.

Nikola Tesla

Perhaps best known (and appreciated!) for his designing the modern AC electricity supply system, Tesla was an inventor who was always looking toward the future to find need. He had the ideas, as he pursued the concept of wireless lighting and wireless intercontinental communication, but he ran out of funding before he could see these inventions through to their end. The press dubbed him a "mad scientist" later in his life, as his bold scientific claims were at the time were unfounded.

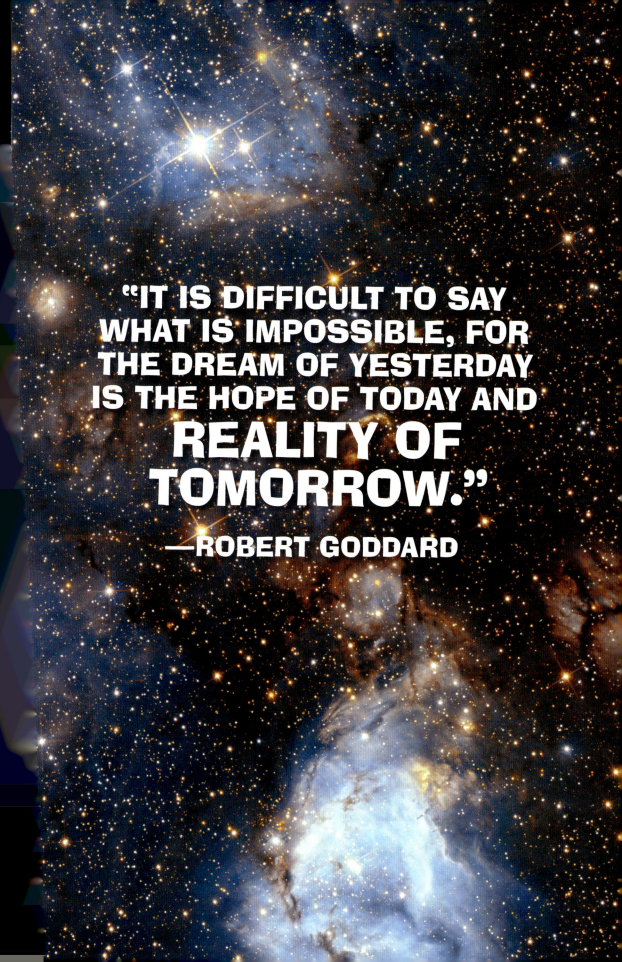

Index

A

Acid? Base? Red Cabbage Can Tell Ya!, 68
Acids
   and bases, 66–67, 68, 98–99
   electricity and, 145
Air expansion, 150–151
Air pressure, 121, 132–133, 136–137, 186–187

Astronomy, 24–25
   The Big Balloon Bang, 38–39
   Dark Side of a Cookie, 30
   Phases of the Moon, 31
   Scale of the Solar System, 34–35
   Sun, Moon, and a Beach Ball, 32–33
   Sundial, 28–29
   Sun Shades, 26–27
   Who's Who in, 40–41
   Why Does the Moon Glow?, 36

B

Bacteria cultivation, 52–53
Balloon Vroom Vroom, 168–169
Bases
   and acids, 66–67, 68, 98–99
   pH and, 82
Basic Binary Numbers, 190
The Big Balloon Bang, 38–39
Binary numbers, 190
Biology, 42–43
   Cultivate Bacteria, 52–53
   Dissect a Turkey, 56–57
   Extract DNA, 46–47
   Model Cell, 50–51
   Naked Egg, 48–49
   Number Estimates, 54
   Rainbow Rose, 55
   Water Filtration, 44–45
   Who's Who in, 58–59
Bohr, Niels, 192
Bonds, chemical, 103, 106
Bottle Balloon, 136–137
Boyle's law, 134–135
Bucket Swing, 156–157
Buoyancy, 127

C

Candy Chromatography, 176
Candy Crush Light, 180–181
Can't You Believe It's Butter?!, 106
Can You Steel the Heat?, 93
Cell, model, 50–51
Centripetal force, 154–155

Chemical bonds, 103, 106
Chemical energy, 70–71, 100–101
Chemistry, 60–61
    Acid? Base? Red Cabbage Can Tell Ya!, 68
    Can't You Believe It's Butter?!, 106
    Can You Steel the Heat?, 93
    CO2 Bubbles, 102
    Colorful Crayons, 88–89
    Density One by One, 84
    Edible Glass, 108
    Egg Geodes, 86
    Elephant Toothpaste, 100–101
    Glow in the Dark Messages, 64–65
    Green Eggs and Ham, 82
    Hand Heating Slime, 94–95
    Ice Cream in a Bag, 110–111
    Instantly Icy, 85
    It's Gold, It's Silver, No! It's Bronze!, 72–73
    Lemony Acid-Base Lemonade, 66–67
    Liar, Liar, Money on Fire!, 76–77
    Lively 60's Lava Lamp, 62–63
    Magnificent Mentos Gravity Geyser, 70–71
    Marvelous Milk Art, 91
    No Cooking, Cooked Egg, 83
    Peanut Butter Poles, 109
    Peep the Marshmallow, 103
    Plastic Milk, 96–97
    Playdough, 90
    Pocket Volcano, 98–99
    Pop Pop Powdered Sherbet, 107
    Rainbow Colored Flames, 74–75
    Rock N Roll Candy, 112–113
    Rubber Bones, 78–79
    Shake it Like a Slushy, 104
    Ski Hands, 92
    Who's Who in, 114–115
Chladni Plates, 142–143
Clear Rainbow, 184
Clouds in a Bottle, 20–21
CO2 Bubbles, 102
Color, 176, 182–183, 184
Colorful Crayons, 88–89
A Compass That Always Points North!, 16
Condensation, 110–111
Conservation of momentum, 165
Crush the Can without the Hulk!, 132–133
Cultivate Bacteria, 52–53
Curie, Marie, 114
Currents, 150–151

D

Dancing Slime, 122–123
Dark Side of a Cookie, 30
Darwin, Charles, 43
Davy, Humphry, 115
Democritus, 61
Density, 84, 186–187
    and polarity, 62–63
Density One by One, 84
Diffraction, 182–183
Dispersed pressure, 160–161
Dissection, turkey, 56–57
DNA extraction, 46–47
Drag, 168–169
Dye, 88–89, 176

E

Earl Grey Ready Rocket, 150–151
Eclipse, solar, 26–27
Edible Glass, 108
Edible Rocks, 12–13
Egg, naked, 48–49
Egg Geodes, 86
Egg in a Bottle, 134–135
Einstein, Albert, 117
Electric Motor, 188–189
Electricity and electric circuits, 144–145, 166–167, 170, 178–179, 188–189
Elephant Toothpaste, 100–101
Energy release, 70–71, 100–101
Estimates, number, 54

Evolution, 43
Expanding Slippery Soap, 147
Expansion
    air, 150–151
    heat, 147, 152–153
    universe, 38–39
Extraction, DNA, 46–47

F

Feverishly Floating Orange, 127
Films, 184
Filtration, water, 44–45
Fleming, Alexander, 58–59
Fluids, non-Newtonian, 120
Forces, 164
Forever Wet Sand, 118
A Fork, a Spoon, and a Toothpick Walk into a Yoga Class, 126
Franklin, Rosalind, 58
Free Falling Egg, 164
Freezing point, 85, 104
Freezing Wire, 158–159
Frequency, 142–143

G

Geodes 101, 87
Geology, 11
    Clouds in a Bottle, 20–21
    A Compass That Always Points North!, 16
    Edible Rocks, 12–13
    Make a Seismograph, 18–19
    Rock Your Rock Knowledge, 17
    Rockin' Rock Cycle, 14–15
    Who's Who in, 22–23

Gilbert, Grove, 11
Glow, moon, 36
Glow in the Dark Messages, 64–65
Gould, Stephen Jay, 59
Gravity, 156–157, 164
Green Eggs and Ham, 82

H
Halley, Edmond, 41
Hand Heating Slime, 94–95
Heat, 172–173
   expansion, 147, 152–153
   solid, 108
   transfer, 94–95
Horology, 28–29
How Much Water Can Lincoln Hold?, 138–139
Hubble, Edwin, 40
Hutton, James, 22

I
Ice Cream in a Bag, 110–111
Inductance, 148–149
Induction, 130
Instantly Icy, 85

Irrational numbers, 171
It's Gold, It's Silver, No! It's Bronze!, 72–73

J
Jell-O in the Dark, 140–141

K
Kepler, Johannes, 40–41
Kinetics, 118
Kwolek, Stephanie, 114

L
Lava lamp, 62–63
Lemon-Lime Power, 145
Lemony Acid-Base Lemonade, 66–67
Lenz's Law, 128
Liar, Liar, Money on Fire!, 76–77
Light, 32–33, 140–141, 180–181
   diffraction, 182–183
   polarization, 177
Liquid properties, 76–77
Lively 60's Lava Lamp, 62–63
Lyell, Charles, 22–23

M

Magnetic fields, 16, 129–131, 148–149
Magnetic Fluid, 131
Magnetic Train, 148–149

Magnification, 174–175
Magnificent Mentos Gravity Geyser, 70–71
Magnifying Heat, 174–175
Make a Seismograph, 18–19
Marvelous Milk Art, 91
Mendel, Gregor, 59
Mendeleev, Dmitri, 114–115
Metals, 74–75
Mini Hovercraft, 186–187
Mixing, 90, 119, 185
Model cell, 50–51
Molecules, nonpolar, 109
Momentum, 165, 168–169
Moon, 11
  glow, 36
  phases of the, 31
Mr. Potato Clock, 166–167

N

Naked Egg, 48–49
Newton, Isaac, 117
Newton's laws, 117, 124–125, 126
No Cooking, Cooked Egg, 83
Nodes, 142–143
Non-Newtonian fluids, 120
Nonpolar molecules, 109
Numbers
  binary, 190
  estimates, 54
  patterns, 191
  Pi, 171

O

Observation, 171
Ooey-Gooey Slime, 120
Organ function, 56–57
Osmosis, 48–49, 55
Out with the Old Paper, In With the New!, 119

P

Patterns, 191
Pauling, Linus, 115

Peanut Butter Poles, 109
Peep the Marshmallow, 103
Periodic Table of Elements, 61, 80–81
pH and base, 82
Phase changes, 112–113
Phases of the Moon, 31
Physical mixing, 119
Physics, 116–117
    Balloon Vroom Vroom, 168–169
    Basic Binary Numbers, 190
    Bottle Balloon, 136–137
    Bucket Swing, 156–157
    Candy Chromatography, 176
    Candy Crush Light, 180–181
    Chladni Plates, 142–143
    Clear Rainbow, 184
    Crush the Can without the Hulk!, 132–133
    Dancing Slime, 122–123
    Earl Grey Ready Rocket, 150–151
    Egg in a Bottle, 134–135
    Electric Motor, 188–189
    Expanding Slippery Soap, 147
    Feverishly Floating Orange, 127
    Forever Wet Sand, 118
    A Fork, a Spoon, and a Toothpick Walk into a Yoga Class, 126
    Free Falling Egg, 164
    Freezing Wire, 158–159
    How Much Water Can Lincoln Hold?, 138–139
    Jell-O in the Dark, 140–141
    Lemon-Lime Power, 145
    Magnetic Fluid, 131
    Magnetic Train, 148–149
    Magnifying Heat, 174–175
    Mini Hovercraft, 186–187
    Mr. Potato Clock, 166–167
    Ooey-Gooey Slime, 120
    Out with the Old Paper, In With the New!, 119
    Pick a Card! Any Card!, 191
    Picky Pi, 171
    Pop Corn on the Cob, 152–153
    Rainbow Reveal, 185
    Rainbow through Water, 182–183
    Rube Goldberg Activity, 165
    Series Circuit, 170
    Simple Circuitry, 144
    Sling Shot Catapult, 162–163
    Solar S'Mores, 172–173

Static Lightning, 178–179
Super Spinning Candle, 124–125
Table Top Spin, 130
3D Polarized, 177
Tornado Twister Tangle, 154–155
Totally Tubular Velocity, 128
Up and Around the Magnet, 129
Walking on Egg Shells, 160–161
Water Rise, 121
Who's Who in, 192–193
Pi (mathematical concept), 171
Pick a Card! Any Card!, 191
Picky Pi, 171
Planets, 32–33
Plastic Milk, 96–97
Playdough, 90
Pocket Volcano, 98–99
Polarity and density, 62–63
Polarization, light, 177
Pop Corn on the Cob, 152–153
Pop Pop Powdered Sherbet, 107
Pressure
   dispersed, 160–161
   temperature and, 158–159

Q
Quantum mechanics, 64–65

R
Rainbow Colored Flames, 74–75
Rainbow Reveal, 185
Rainbow Rose, 55
Rainbow through Water, 182–183
Rockin' Rock Cycle, 14–15
Rock N Roll Candy, 112–113
Rock Your Rock Knowledge, 17
Rocks
   edible, 12–13
   formation, 12–13
   knowledge, 17
   layers, 14–15
Rubber Bones, 78–79
Rube Goldberg Activity, 165
Rubin, Vera, 40
Rutherford, Ernest, 193

S
Sagan, Carl, 41
Scale of the Solar System, 34–35

Schmitt, Harrison, 11, 23
Schrödinger, Erwin, 193
Science, what is, 8
Science experiments, safety as most important thing in, 9
Scientist Profiles, 37, 69, 146
Seismograph, 18–19
Series Circuit, 170
Shake it Like a Slushy, 104
Simple Circuitry, 144
Ski Hands, 92
Sling Shot Catapult, 162–163
Smith, William, 23
Solar eclipse, 26–27
Solar S'Mores, 172–173
Solar system, scale of the, 34–35
Sound waves, 122–123
States of Matter, 105
Static Lightning, 178–179
Stored chemical energy, 92
Sublimation, 102
Sun, Moon, and a Beach Ball, 32–33
Sundial, 28–29
Sun Shades, 26–27
Supernovas, 25
Super Spinning Candle, 124–125
Surface tension, 91, 138–139

T

Table Top Spin, 130
Tectonic plates, 18–19
Temperature and pressure, 158–159
Tesla, Nikola, 193
Tharp, Marie, 22
Thermodynamics, 134–135

3D Polarized, 177
Time, 28–29, 32–33
Tornado Twister Tangle, 154–155
Totally Tubular Velocity, 128
Trajectory, 162–163
Turkey Dissection, 56–57

U

Universe expansion, 38–39
Up and Around the Magnet, 129

V

Visibility, 36

W

Walking on Egg Shells, 160–161
Wallace, Alfred Russell, 58
Water Filtration, 44–45
Water Rise, 121
Who's Who
    in astronomy, 40–41
    in chemistry, 114–115
    in geology, 22–23
    in physics, 192–193
Wu, Chien-Shiung, 192

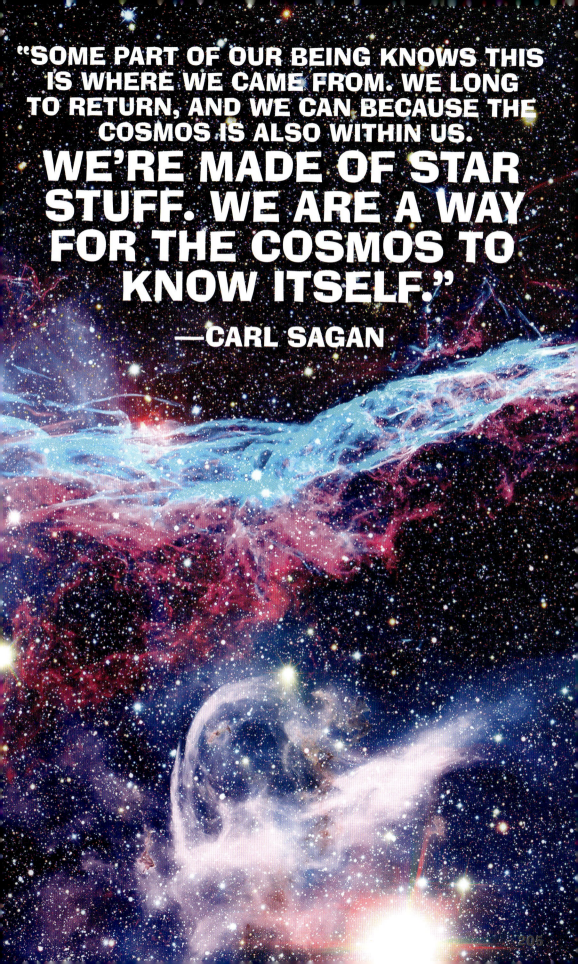

ABOUT THE ILLUSTRATOR

Steve Björkman has illustrated more than 70 books for children, including picture books such as Good Night, Little One, easy readers such as Thanksgiving Is..., and series such as Mama Rex and T. Steve is also well known for illustrating greeting cards. More than 100 million of his greeting cards for Recycled Paper Greetings have been sold.

ABOUT THE AUTHOR

Haley Fica lives in New York City. She is working towards her Master's degree in Mechanical Engineering at Columbia University. She has researched for the American Museum of Natural History's astrophysics department under the direction of three women scientists and the research group Brown Dwarfs of New York City. She also worked at Carnegie Observatories in Pasadena. She hopes to one day build telescopes or rockets in order to continue exploring the universe around her.

About Applesauce Press

Good ideas ripen with time. From seed to harvest, Applesauce Press crafts books with beautiful designs, creative formats, and kid-friendly information on a variety of fascinating topics. Like our parent company, Cider Mill Press Book Publishers, our press bears fruit twice a year, publishing a new crop of titles each spring and fall.

Write to us at:
PO Box 454
Kennebunkport, ME 04046

Or visit us on the web at: www.cidermillpress.com

Whalen Book Works is a book packaging company that combines top-notch design, unique formats, and fresh content to create truly innovative gift books. We plant one tree for every 10 books we print, and your purchase supports a tree in the Rocky Mountain National Park.

NEW YORK CITY, NEW YORK

Visit us on the web at
www.whalenbooks.com or
write to us at
338 E 100 Street, Suite 5A
New York, NY 10029